"*The Totally Unbelievable Collection Of Incredibly Delicious American Classics Cookbook* features mouthwatering recipes for more than 100 favorite American meals. Together, Karen and I picked the most popular, tantalizing, all-time everyday classics! Then I asked her to create the most delicious version of each. The result is this cookbook masterpiece jam-packed with the best of the best of the best meals you'll find anywhere."
"Whatever the mood or the occasion, we're sure you'll find the perfect recipe right here. We're also sure you'll find it absolutely mouthwatering delicious."
Jerry Jerome
Jerry Jerome
The guy behind The Turkey Store®
Karen Levin
The gal behind The Cookbook
THE TURKEY STORE
FRESH TURKEY
Lean Ground
THE TURKEY STORE
FRESH TURKEY
Breast Slices
Karen Levin has more than 20 years of experience and 30 cookbook titles to her name and contributes articles to a variety of monthly publications including *Cooking Light*, *Better Homes & Gardens*, *Vegetarian Times* and *Health* magazine. In addition, she teaches a variety of cooking classes in the Chicago area, consults with numerous food companies, and writes a weekly internet column for the Chicago Tribune.

TABLE OF CONTENTS

FOOD FOR THOUGHT

MEATLOAF RECIPES

Did You Know That?

Meatloaf has been an American favorite for at least 100 years. The first meatloaf recipe appeared in print in 1899 (according to John Mariani, The Dictionary of American Food and Drink).

Menu Makers

Best Ever Meatloaf calls for potatoes, so serve with boiled red potatoes or mashed or baked russet potatoes. (Potatoes can bake along with the meatloaf if you put them in the preheated oven 30 minutes beforehand.) Round out the menu with your favorite green and yellow vegetables in season: green peas, green beans, asparagus, squash, corn, or carrots. That adds up to three of the recommended five daily servings of fruits and vegetables—and it makes a colorful plate. Grilled Meatloaf, corn on the cob and fruit kabobs make a nice trio. What could be better with Italian Style meatloaf than a huge green salad and crusty Italian bread?

Tips and Tricks

• To minimize cracking during baking, rub top of meatloaf with cold water until smooth before putting it in the oven. To avoid any unattractive "holes" in meatloaf bottom, press mixture firmly into loaf pan corners and bottom in layers using a rubber spatula.

• To be sure meatloaf is done, check with meat thermometer. It should register 160°F in center. Temperature will rise to 170°F after meatloaf is removed from oven.

• Let meatloaf rest 10 to 15 minutes in the pan after baking to firm up and ensure easy slicing.

• Double recipe and bake two meatloaves—one for now and one to freeze for another day. Defrost the night before in the refrigerator.

• Fancy top: Before placing on serving platter, sprinkle top evenly with one or a combination of chopped Italian parsley, grated hard-boiled egg, finely chopped tomatoes or criss-cross with canned, drained and julienned roasted red peppers or fresh chives.

• Bake individual meatloaves in large muffin pans sprayed with non-stick spray. Bake for 25 minutes or until meat thermometer registers 170°F.

• Leftovers? Slice cold meatloaf thickly for sandwiches on white or rye bread with mustard or mayonnaise, lettuce and sliced tomato. Slice cold meatloaf thinly and serve with melba toast, Dijon mustard and cornichons for an appetizer.

MEATLOAF
RECIPES
M

BEST EVER MEATLOAF

2 tablespoons butter or margarine
1 cup chopped onion
3 cloves garlic, minced
1 pkg. The Turkey Store® Lean Ground
½ cup fresh bread crumbs
1 large egg
¾ cup catsup
2 teaspoons Worcestershire sauce
¾ teaspoon salt
½ teaspoon freshly ground black pepper

Heat oven to 350 degrees. Melt butter in a small skillet over medium-high heat. Add onion and garlic; cook 5 minutes, stirring occasionally. Transfer mixture to a large bowl; cool 5 minutes.

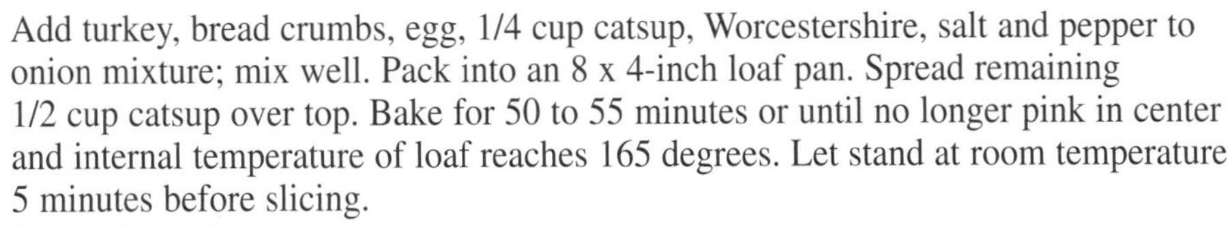
Add turkey, bread crumbs, egg, 1/4 cup catsup, Worcestershire, salt and pepper to onion mixture; mix well. Pack into an 8 x 4-inch loaf pan. Spread remaining 1/2 cup catsup over top. Bake for 50 to 55 minutes or until no longer pink in center and internal temperature of loaf reaches 165 degrees. Let stand at room temperature 5 minutes before slicing.

Makes 5 servings.

Nutrition information per serving: Calories: 243, Protein: 30g, Carbohydrates: 16g, Fat: 7g, Cholesterol: 110mg, Sodium: 890mg

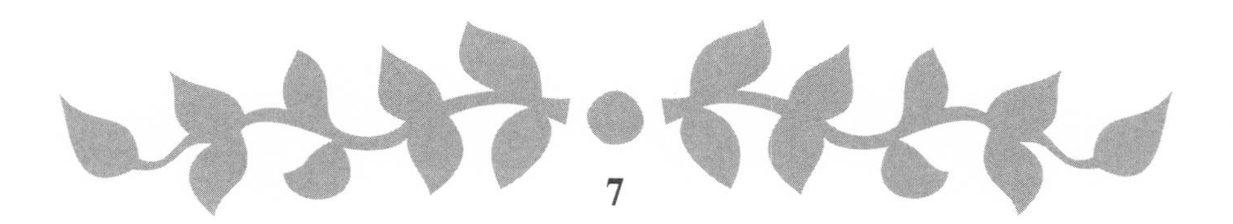

ITALIAN MEATLOAF

1 pkg. The Turkey Store® Lean Ground
1 pkg. The Turkey Store® Hot or Sweet Lean Italian Sausage, casings removed
½ cup fresh bread crumbs
1 large egg
1 cup prepared tomato and basil spaghetti sauce
1 clove garlic, minced
¾ teaspoon salt
½ teaspoon freshly ground black pepper

Heat oven to 350 degrees. In a large bowl, combine ground turkey, turkey sausage, bread crumbs, egg, 1/2 cup spaghetti sauce, garlic, salt and pepper; mix well. On a 15 x 10-inch jelly roll pan, shape mixture into a loaf about 10 x 6 inches. Spread remaining 1/2 cup spaghetti sauce over top. Bake for 1 hour or until no longer pink in center and internal temperature of loaf reaches 165 degrees. Let stand at room temperature 5 minutes before slicing.

Makes 8 servings.

Nutrition information per serving: Calories: 193, Protein: 27g, Carbohydrates: 5g, Fat: 7g, Cholesterol: 89mg, Sodium: 785mg

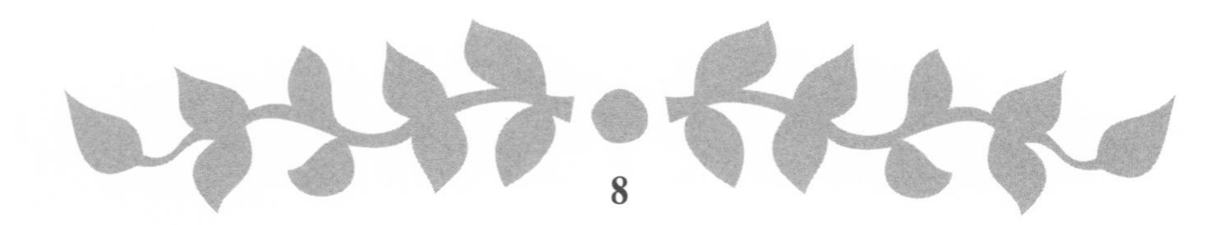

GRILLED MEATLOAF

- 1 pkg. The Turkey Store® Lean Ground
- ⅓ cup finely chopped onion
- ⅓ cup seasoned dry bread crumbs
- ⅔ cup chili sauce
- 1 egg
- ½ teaspoon salt
- ½ teaspoon freshly ground black pepper
- ½ teaspoon dried sage
- 2 tablespoons packed brown sugar
- 1 tablespoon horseradish mustard or Dijon mustard

In a large bowl, combine turkey, onion, bread crumbs, 1/3 cup chili sauce, egg, salt, pepper and sage; mix well. On a large plate, shape mixture into a 8 x 4-inch oval loaf about 1-1/2 inches thick. Cover and chill at least 30 minutes or up to 8 hours.

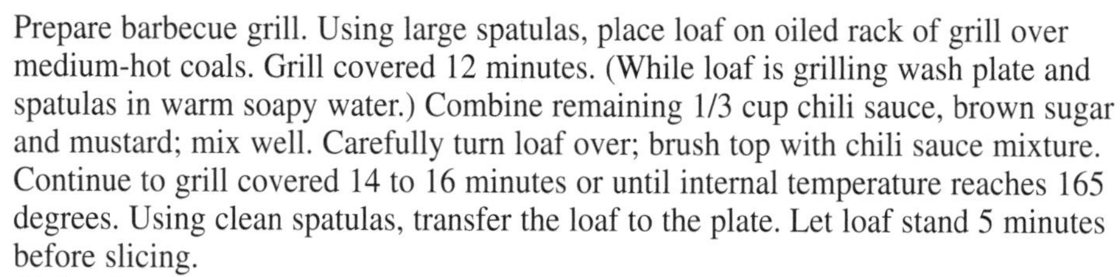

Prepare barbecue grill. Using large spatulas, place loaf on oiled rack of grill over medium-hot coals. Grill covered 12 minutes. (While loaf is grilling wash plate and spatulas in warm soapy water.) Combine remaining 1/3 cup chili sauce, brown sugar and mustard; mix well. Carefully turn loaf over; brush top with chili sauce mixture. Continue to grill covered 14 to 16 minutes or until internal temperature reaches 165 degrees. Using clean spatulas, transfer the loaf to the plate. Let loaf stand 5 minutes before slicing.

Makes 5 servings.

Nutrition information per serving: Calories: 261, Protein: 26g, Carbohydrates: 19g, Fat: 10g, Cholesterol: 113mg, Sodium: 1,057mg

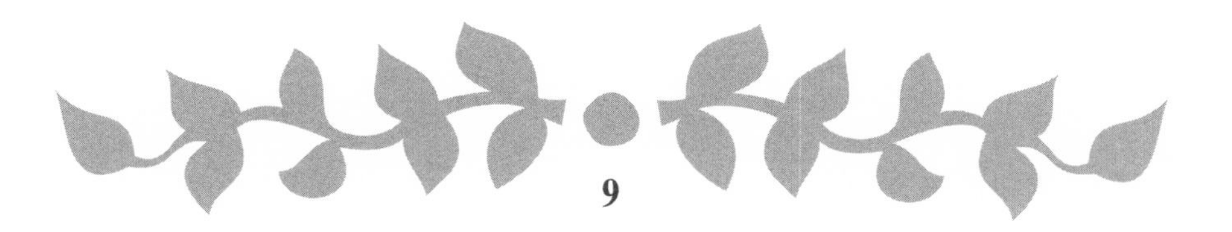

Light Best Ever Meatloaf

Cooking spray
1 cup chopped onion
3 cloves garlic, minced
1 pkg. The Turkey Store® Extra Lean Ground Breast
½ cup fresh bread crumbs
1 large egg white
¾ cup catsup
2 teaspoons Worcestershire sauce
¾ teaspoon salt (optional)
½ teaspoon freshly ground black pepper

MEATLOAF RECIPES

Heat oven to 350 degrees. Coat a small skillet with cooking spray; place over medium-high heat. Add onion and garlic; cook 5 minutes, stirring occasionally. Transfer mixture to a large bowl; cool 5 minutes.

Add turkey, bread crumbs, egg white, 1/4 cup catsup, Worcestershire, salt and pepper to onion mixture; mix well. Pack into an 8 x 4-inch loaf pan. Spread remaining 1/2 cup catsup over top. Bake for 50 to 55 minutes or until no longer pink in center and internal temperature of loaf reaches 165 degrees. Let stand at room temperature 5 minutes before slicing.

Makes 5 servings.

Nutrition information per serving: Calories: 191, Protein: 29g, Carbohydrates: 16g, Fat: 2g, Cholesterol: 55mg, Sodium: 568mg

SPAGHETTI RECIPES

Did You Know That?

• Dried pasta (often just called macaroni) was a favorite American food by Civil War days. A recipe for Macaroni a l'Italienne in Mrs. Rorer's Philadelphia Cook Book, 1886, informs readers that "Spighetti [author's spelling] is the most delicate form of macaroni that comes to this country."
• Spaghetti, like all eggless dried pasta, is a low-calorie carbohydrate choice because of its ability to absorb water as it cooks; it doubles in volume.

Menu Makers

• With more than 300 pasta shapes to choose from, don't just stick to spaghetti—except for Spaghetti with Meatballs (an Italian-American classic). Try mostaccioli with meat sauce or sliced cooked Italian sausage and sauce over bow-tie pasta. Tri-colored pasta shells make a nice change of pace and spinach linguini adds extra color and flavor. Whole wheat pasta, available now in many supermarkets, has more protein and fiber than pasta made from white durum flour.
• When it comes to making a complete meal, you can even skip the Italian bread and just add a big green salad. For ultimate convenience, open a bag of ready-to-eat Italian mixed greens and toss with your favorite Italian dressing.

Tips and Tricks

• Purchase pasta made from hard durum wheat flour (semolina) without eggs.
• Use about four quarts of water to cook every pound of pasta. Always add salt to water after it comes to a boil; salted water takes longer to boil.
• Try cooking pasta al dente (or a little firm to the teeth) according to package directions. Overcooked pasta loses nutrients. Cover the pot after putting pasta into boiling water so temperature rises again quickly. Uncover pot after water returns to a boil and stir once to prevent sticking.
• Never rinse cooked pasta with water; just drain well. The residual starch helps keep the sauce from slipping off the pasta.
• Leftover pasta mixed with sauce? Refrigerate covered. Reheat in microwave safe dish covered with a sheet of waxed paper.
• Leftover sauce? Refrigerate covered up to three days or freeze up to three months.

SPAGHETTI
RECIPES

HOMESTYLE SPAGHETTI AND MEATBALLS

SPAGHETTI RECIPES

SPAGHETTI SAUCE

- 2 tablespoons olive oil
- 1 cup chopped onion
- 4 cloves garlic, minced
- 2 cans (28 oz.) Italian-style plum tomatoes, undrained, coarsely chopped
- 1 can (6 oz.) tomato paste
- 1-½ teaspoons dried basil
- 1 teaspoon dried oregano
- 1 teaspoon sugar
- ½ teaspoon salt
- ¼ teaspoon crushed red pepper flakes (optional)
- 12 oz. spaghetti or thin spaghetti, cooked and drained
- ¼ cup grated Parmesan or Romano cheese

Heat oil in a large saucepan over medium-high heat. Add onion; cook 5 minutes, stirring occasionally. Add garlic; cook 2 minutes. Add tomatoes, tomato paste, basil, oregano, sugar, salt and, if desired, pepper flakes; bring to a simmer. Simmer uncovered 25 to 35 minutes or until sauce is desired consistency.

MEATBALLS

- 1 recipe homestyle tomato sauce (see recipe above)
- 1 pkg. The Turkey Store® Lean Ground
- ¼ cup seasoned dry bread crumbs
- 1 large egg
- ¾ teaspoon dried basil
- ¾ teaspoon garlic salt
- ¼ teaspoon freshly ground black pepper
- 1 tablespoon olive oil

Prepare spaghetti sauce as recipe directs. While sauce is simmering, combine all ingredients for meatballs in a large bowl. Mix well and shape into about 24 1-inch meatballs. Heat oil in a large nonstick skillet over high heat until hot. Add meatballs; reduce heat to medium and cook until browned on all sides, about 12 minutes, turning occasionally. Add to simmering sauce; cook uncovered about 10 minutes or until meatballs are no longer pink in center. Serve over hot cooked spaghetti; sprinkle with Parmesan cheese.
Makes 6 servings.

Nutrition information per serving: Calories: 565, Protein: 35g, Carbohydrates: 70mg, Fat: 18g, Cholesterol: 97mg, Sodium: 1,275mg

Spaghetti With Hot Italian Sausage

SAUCE

- 2 tablespoons olive oil
- 1 cup chopped onion
- 4 cloves garlic, minced
- 2 cans (28 oz.) Italian-style plum tomatoes, undrained, coarsely chopped
- 1 can (6 oz.) tomato paste
- 1-½ teaspoons dried basil
- 1 teaspoon dried oregano
- 1 teaspoon sugar
- ½ teaspoon salt
- ¼ teaspoon crushed red pepper flakes (optional)
- 1 pkg. The Turkey Store® Hot Italian Sausage
- 12 oz. spaghetti or thin spaghetti, cooked and drained
- ¼ cup grated Parmesan or Romano cheese
- Chopped basil (optional)

Prepare spaghetti sauce as recipe on page 13 directs. While sauce is simmering, cook Italian sausage according to package directions. Cut sausage into 1/2-inch slices, remove casings and cook in a nonstick skillet over medium-high heat until no longer pink in center, 8 to 10 minutes, stirring occasionally. Serve whole sausages over spaghetti and sauce or stir sliced cooked sausage into sauce and heat through. Sprinkle with chopped basil, if desired and serve with grated Parmesan cheese.

Makes 6 servings.

Nutrition information per serving: Calories: 491, Protein: 25g, Carbohydrates: 67g, Fat: 14g, Cholesterol: 41mg, Sodium: 1,470mg

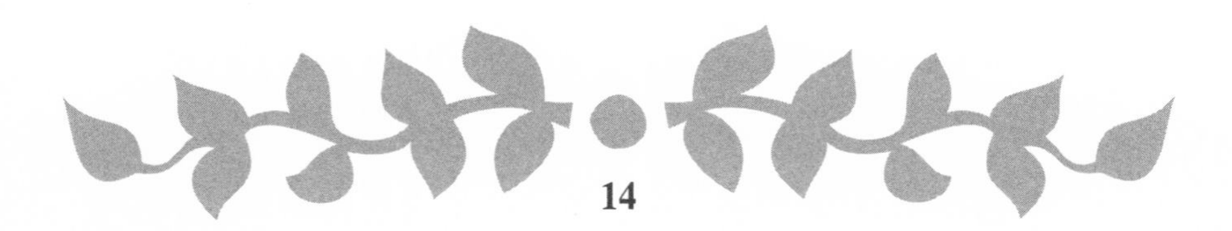

TEX-MEX SPAGHETTI

- 1 pkg. The Turkey Store® Smoke Seasoned Lean Sausage or Lean Bratwurst
- 1 cup chopped onion
- 2 teaspoons bottled or fresh minced garlic
- 1 tablespoon Mexican seasoning or 2 teaspoons chili powder plus 1 teaspoon ground cumin
- 1 can (14-½ oz.) chili- or salsa-style tomatoes, undrained
- ¾ cup picante sauce
- 1 teaspoon dried oregano
- 1-½ cups (6 oz.) shredded Mexican or cheddar cheese
- 12 oz. spaghetti, cooked and drained

Crumble sausage into a large saucepan; discard casings. Add onion, garlic and Mexican seasoning; cook over medium-high heat 8 minutes, stirring occasionally. Add tomatoes, picante sauce and oregano; bring to a boil. Reduce heat; simmer uncovered 15 to 20 minutes or until thickened. Transfer spaghetti to serving plates. Top with sauce; sprinkle with cheese.
Makes 6 servings.

Nutrition information per serving: Calories: 491, Protein: 27g, Carbohydrates: 55g, Fat: 18g, Cholesterol: 80mg, Sodium: 1,241mg

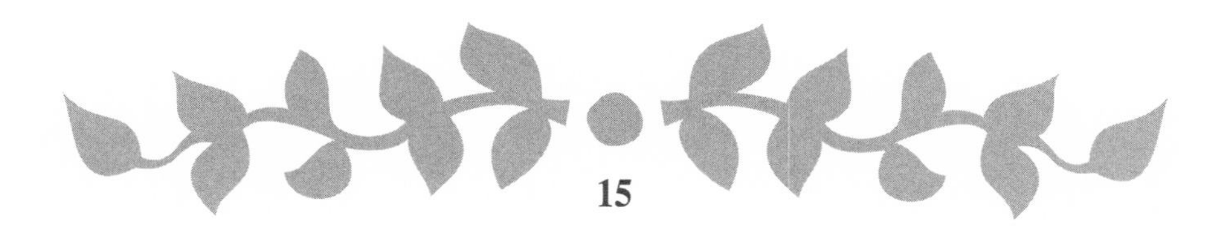

Light Spaghetti With Meat Sauce

Cooking spray
1 cup chopped onion
4 cloves garlic, minced
2 cans (28 oz.) Italian style plum tomatoes, undrained, coarsely chopped
1 can (6 oz.) tomato paste
1-½ teaspoons dried basil
1 teaspoon dried oregano
1 teaspoon sugar
½ teaspoon salt (optional)
¼ teaspoon crushed red pepper flakes (optional)
1 pkg. The Turkey Store® Extra Lean Ground Breast
12 oz. spaghetti or thin spaghetti, cooked and drained
2 tablespoons grated Parmesan or Romano cheese

Coat a large saucepan with cooking spray; heat over medium-high heat. Add onion; cook 5 minutes, stirring occasionally. Add garlic; cook 2 minutes. Add tomatoes, tomato paste, basil, oregano, sugar and, if desired, salt and pepper flakes; bring to a simmer. Simmer uncovered 25 to 35 minutes or until sauce is desired consistency.

Meanwhile, cook turkey in a large skillet just until no longer pink, breaking into chunks with a wooden spoon. Stir turkey into sauce; heat through. Serve over spaghetti and sprinkle with cheese.

Makes 6 servings.

Nutrition information per serving: Calories: 425, Protein: 35g, Carbohydrates: 65g, Fat: 4g, Cholesterol: 47mg, Sodium: 758mg

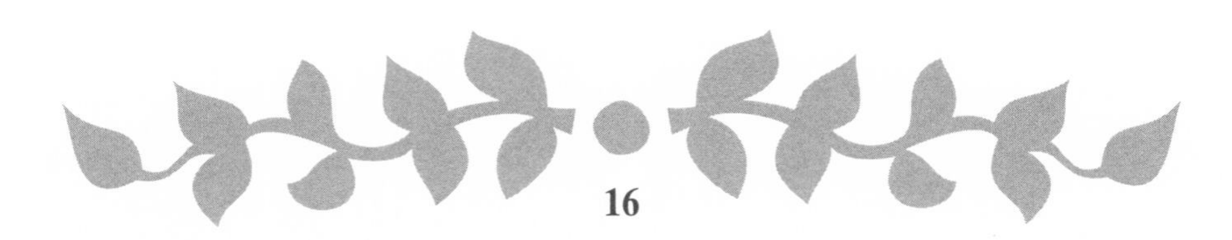

FOOD FOR THOUGHT

BURGER RECIPES

Did You Know That?

Americans invented the hamburger, alright, but which American? Take your pick of the following, each credited with the honor:

- First, Delmonico's Restaurant in New York listed "hamburger steak" on its 1936 menu—the first printed menu in America.
- Second, Charles Nagreen, 15-year-old concessionaire at the 1883 Seymour, Wisconsin County Fair, placed his butter-fried ground beef between bread slices so customers could eat while strolling around the fair.
- Third, Akron, Ohio County Fair concessionaire Frank Menches, 27, ran out of sausage for sandwiches, so he ground up meat and served it as a meat patty.
- And last, Louis Lassen, owner of Louis' Lunch Counter in New Haven, Connecticut, ground lean beef, broiled it and served it between two slices of toast.

By 1912, ground meat patties on soft yeast buns were becoming increasingly popular, and shortly thereafter "burger" was used to describe other ground meats such as lamb, chicken, and even clams. In the 1970s, the veggie burger made its appearance. The latest and perhaps tastiest burger to make the scene is the turkey burger.

Menu Makers

- Burgers and fries are natural go-togethers. But rather than deep-fried fries, try easy oven fries. For four servings, scrub 2 large russet potatoes and cut each into 16 somewhat equal lengthwise skin-on strips. Toss strips in bowl with 1 Tbsp. canola or olive oil to coat. Spread in single layer on baking sheet lightly sprayed with vegetable oil spray. Sprinkle lightly with salt and pepper. Bake in preheated 425°F oven for 25 minutes or until cooked through and browned. Remove with spatula.
- For a no-fuss burger lunch or supper, add potato chips and your choice of coleslaw, carrot-raisin salad or three-bean salad from the deli.
- Try baked taco chips with the Mexicali Burger.

Tips and Tricks

- Combine ground turkey mixture with a large spoon or spatula, not with hands. The heat from your hands alters the texture of the burger.
- Never press down on patties while they're cooking with a spatula; that will force out juices.
- To keep meat from sticking, moisten hands with cold water before shaping patties.
- Patties are easier to form if you chill the mixture first.
- To ensure a light texture in cooked burgers, don't overmix ground turkey. Stir until ingredients are just combined.
- Food safety: don't put cooked burgers back on the plate used for uncooked burgers.

BURGER
RECIPES
B

ALL-AMERICAN CHEESEBURGERS

- 1 pkg. The Turkey Store® Lean Ground
- ⅓ cup catsup
- 3 tablespoons seasoned dry bread crumbs
- 2 tablespoons grated or finely chopped onion
- 1 large egg
- ½ teaspoon garlic salt
- ¼ teaspoon freshly ground black pepper
- 4 slices (¼ inch) red or yellow onion
- Cooking spray
- 4 slices cheddar cheese
- 4 kaiser rolls or bakery-style hamburger buns, split
- 4 slices tomato
- 4 leaves romaine or red leaf lettuce
- Optional condiments: mayonnaise, catsup, mustard, sliced pickles

BURGER RECIPES

In a large bowl, combine turkey, catsup, bread crumbs, onion, egg, garlic salt and pepper. Mix well and shape into 4 patties about 1/2-inch thick. Cover and refrigerate while preparing charcoal grill. Coat patties and onion slices with cooking spray. Grill patties and onions over medium coals 6 to 7 minutes per side or until no longer pink in center. Top patties with cheese during last minute of grilling. Place rolls, cut side down on grill during last 1 to 2 minutes of cooking to toast lightly. Serve patties in rolls topped with grilled onions, tomato and lettuce. Serve with desired condiments.

Makes 4 servings.

Nutrition information per serving: Calories: 566, Protein: 45g, Carbohydrates: 49g, Fat: 23g, Cholesterol: 171mg, Sodium: 1,188mg

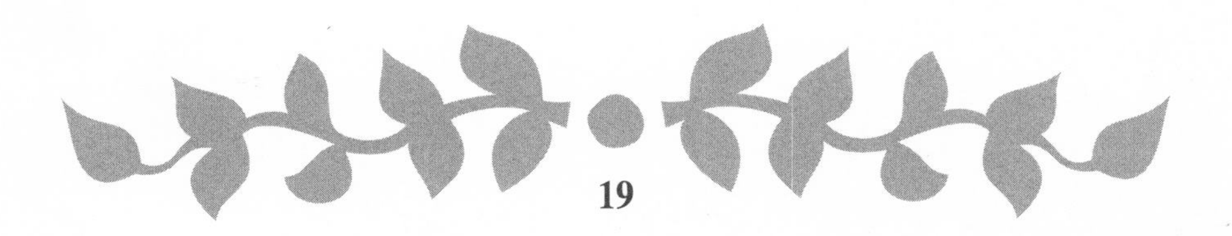

MEXICALI BURGERS

- 1 ripe avocado, peeled, seeded and diced
- ⅓ cup thick and chunky salsa
- 2 tablespoons chopped cilantro or green onions
- 1 pkg. The Turkey Store® Lightly Seasoned Extra Lean Breast Patties
- 4 slices Monterey jack cheese with jalapeño peppers (optional)
- 4 kaiser rolls or hamburger buns, split, toasted if desired
- 4 red leaf or romaine lettuce leaves

Prepare barbecue grill or preheat broiler. In a small bowl, combine avocado, salsa and cilantro or green onions; set aside. Grill or broil patties about 5 inches from heat source 3 to 4 minutes per side or until no longer pink in center. If desired, place cheese over patties during the last minute of cooking. Place lettuce on bottom of rolls; top with patties and avocado mixture and close with roll tops.
Makes 4 servings.

Nutrition information per serving: Calories: 450, Protein: 29g, Carbohydrates: 46g, Fat: 18g, Cholesterol: 70mg, Sodium: 1,193mg

MOUTH-WATERING PATTY MELTS

- 2 tablespoons butter or margarine
- 1 cup chopped onion
- 1 pkg. The Turkey Store® Lean Burger Patties
- ¾ teaspoon salt
- ¼ teaspoon freshly ground black pepper
- 8 slices rye or pumpernickel bread
- 8 slices American or cheddar cheese

Melt 1 tablespoon butter in a large nonstick skillet over medium heat. Add onion; cook 10 minutes or until tender and golden brown, stirring occasionally. Meanwhile, preheat broiler. Sprinkle burger patties with salt and pepper. Broil 4 to 5 inches from heat source 3 to 4 minutes per side or until no longer pink in center. Place 1 slice of cheese over each slice of bread. Place burger patties over 4 slices bread; top with onions. Close sandwiches with remaining bread, cheese side down. Melt 1/2 tablespoon butter in same skillet. Cook 2 sandwiches at a time in skillet until browned and cheese is melted, about 3 minutes per side. Repeat with remaining butter and 2 sandwiches.

Makes 4 servings.

Nutrition information per serving: Calories: 494, Protein: 35g, Carbohydrates: 31g, Fat: 26g, Cholesterol: 112mg, Sodium: 1,370mg

GRILLED BURGERS SUPREME

1 pkg. The Turkey Store® Seasoned Lean Burger Patties
Cooking spray
4 slices muenster, provolone or cheddar cheese (optional)
4 onion or bakery-style hamburger rolls, split, toasted or grilled if desired
4 red leaf or romaine lettuce leaves
4 thin slices red onion
4 slices tomato
Optional condiments: catsup, mustard, mayonnaise and sliced pickles

Prepare barbecue grill. Coat patties with cooking spray. Grill over medium coals 3 to 4 minutes per side or until no longer pink in center. If desired, place cheese over patties during last minute of cooking. Top bottom of rolls with lettuce, grilled patties, onion and tomato slices and top of rolls. Serve with desired condiments.
Makes 4 servings.

Nutrition information per serving: Calories: 320, Protein: 26g, Carbohydrates: 30g, Fat: 10g, Cholesterol: 70mg, Sodium: 935mg

ITALIAN BURGERS

- 1 pkg. The Turkey Store® Lean Ground
- ⅓ cup plus 3 tablespoons prepared pizza or spaghetti sauce
- ⅓ cup Italian-seasoned bread crumbs
- 1 egg
- ¼ cup chopped pitted Kalamata or ripe olives
- 1 teaspoon dried basil
- ½ teaspoon garlic salt
- ¼ teaspoon crushed red pepper flakes or freshly ground black pepper
- 4 slices provolone cheese
- 4 hamburger buns, split
- 2 tablespoons Italian dressing
- 8 large spinach leaves or 4 romaine lettuce leaves (optional)

In a large bowl, combine turkey, 1/3 cup pizza sauce, bread crumbs, egg, olives, basil, garlic salt and pepper flakes; mix well. Shape into 4 patties about 1/2-inch thick. Cover and refrigerate while preparing charcoal grill.

Grill patties over medium coals 6 minutes per side. Top patties with remaining pizza sauce and cheese. Brush cut sides of buns with dressing; place cut sides down on grill. Continue to grill 2 minutes or until burgers are no longer pink in center and buns are lightly toasted. Serve burgers in buns with spinach, if desired.

Makes 4 servings.

Nutrition information per serving: Calories: 498, Protein: 49g, Carbohydrates: 35g, Fat: 19g, Cholesterol: 147mg, Sodium: 1,182mg

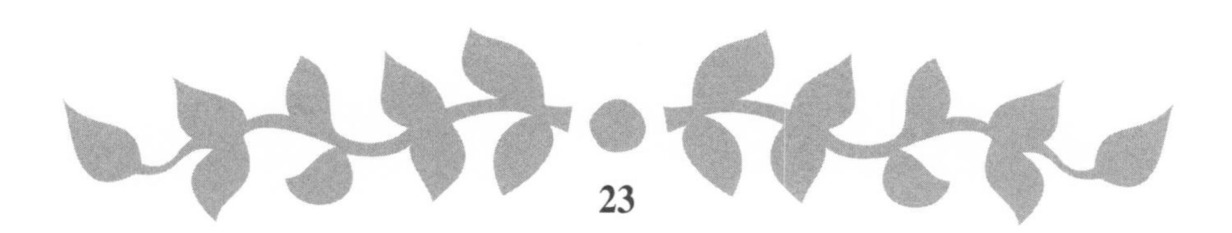

Light All-American Cheeseburgers

- 1 pkg. The Turkey Store® Extra Lean Ground Breast
- ⅓ cup catsup
- 3 tablespoons seasoned dry bread crumbs
- 2 tablespoons grated or finely chopped onion
- 1 egg white
- ½ teaspoon garlic salt (optional)
- ¼ teaspoon freshly ground black pepper
- 4 slices (¼-inch) red or yellow onion
- Cooking spray
- 4 slices fat-free American cheese
- 4 kaiser rolls, split
- 4 slices tomato
- 4 leaves romaine or red leaf lettuce
- Optional condiments: mayonnaise, catsup, mustard, sliced pickles

BURGER RECIPES

In a large bowl, combine turkey, catsup, bread crumbs, onion, egg white, garlic salt and pepper. Mix well and shape into 4 patties about 1/2-inch thick. Cover and refrigerate while preparing charcoal grill.

Coat patties and onion slices with cooking spray. Grill patties and onions over medium coals 6 to 7 minutes per side or until no longer pink in center. Top patties with cheese during last minute of grilling. Place rolls cut side down on grill during last 1 to 2 minutes of cooking to toast lightly. Serve patties in rolls topped with grilled onions, tomato and lettuce. Serve with desired condiments.

Makes 4 servings.

Nutrition information per serving: Calories: 378, Protein: 46g, Carbohydrates: 44g, Fat: 3g, Cholesterol: 69mg, Sodium: 1,084mg

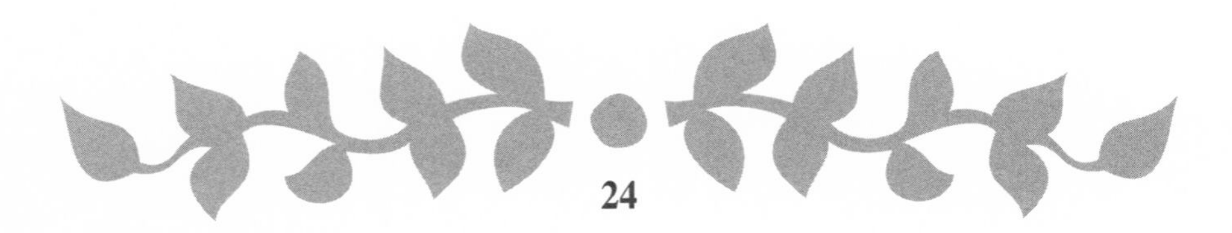

FOOD FOR THOUGHT

TACO RECIPES

Did You Know That?

Tortilla means "little cake," and that's exactly what a tortilla is—a flat unleavened little cake made from corn or wheat flour and baked on a griddle. The corn tortilla is the ancient bread of Mexico, made centuries before the Spanish conquistadors discovered it (along with chocolate) at the court of Montezuma. The Spanish brought wheat to the New World, and soon it was being used to make flour tortillas. Tacos—filled and either folded or rolled tortillas—are snack foods in Mexico. But American Tex-Mex cookery has transformed them into complete meals.

Menu Makers

• For a satisfying and easy Tex-Mex plate, add a side of refried beans and yellow rice to tacos. Refried beans are available in cans and rice can be quickly made from a rice mix.

• For any chili fan, serve bottled red pepper sauce so they can turn up the heat on their tacos.

• Alternative sides: instead of refried beans and rice, serve corn and squash, two native American vegetables. Try corn on the cob and baked acorn squash, or Mexican corn (corn kernels with diced red and green bell pepper) and winter squash puree (available frozen).

• For a lighter meal, serve tacos with a fresh spinach salad mixed with thinly sliced red onions and canned drained Mandarin orange segments.

• For soft tacos, follow taco recipe directions, but spoon taco mixture on one half of soft tortilla and fold the other half on top.

• Try whole wheat flour tortillas for a flavorful soft taco variation.

Tips and Tricks

• To keep flour tortillas from cracking, soften by heating briefly on both sides in a preheated dry skillet. Stack tortillas under a clean napkin to keep soft and warm until ready to fill.

• Leftover tortillas? Don't discard. Cut into 8 wedges and bake until crisp and lightly browned—but not burned—on a baking sheet in a 350°F oven. Use with extra salsa for dipping and snacking.

• Leftover taco filling? Refrigerate covered. For microwavable nachos, spread tortilla chips on microwave-safe plate, dot with filling, top with shredded Monterey jack or jalapeño jack cheese and microwave until cheese melts and filling is hot. Some like them hot, so offer sliced jalapeños on the side.

TACO
RECIPES

TANTALIZING TACOS

- 1 tablespoon vegetable oil
- 1 medium onion, chopped
- 1 green bell pepper, chopped
- 3 cloves garlic, minced
- 1 pkg. The Turkey Store® Lean Ground
- 1 tablespoon chili powder
- 1 teaspoon ground cumin
- ¾ teaspoon salt
- ¾ cup prepared salsa
- 12 taco shells or soft flour tortillas
- 1-½ cups (6 oz.) shredded cheddar or Monterey jack cheese
- 1-½ cups shredded lettuce
- 1 cup chopped tomato
- Optional toppings: sour cream, chopped cilantro, diced avocado, additional salsa

Heat oil in a large skillet over medium-high heat. Add onion, green pepper and garlic; cook 4 minutes, stirring occasionally. Crumble turkey into skillet; sprinkle with chili powder, cumin and salt. Cook 5 minutes or until turkey is no longer pink, stirring frequently. Add salsa; simmer 10 to 12 minutes or until sauce thickens. Spoon 1/3 cup mixture into each taco shell; top with cheese, lettuce and tomato. Serve with desired toppings.

Makes 6 servings.

Nutrition information per serving: Calories: 413, Protein: 33g, Carbohydrates: 29g, Fat: 20g, Cholesterol: 76mg, Sodium: 889

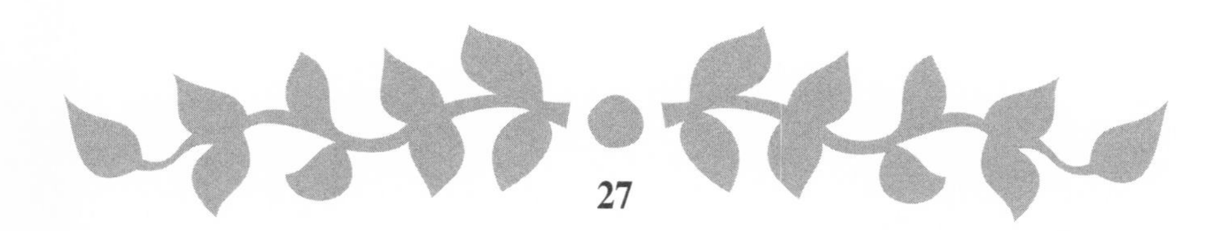

CHUNKY SANTA FE TACOS

- 1 pkg. The Turkey Store® Boneless Breast Tenderloins
- 1 tablespoon chili powder
- 1 teaspoon ground cumin
- ¾ teaspoon salt
- 1 tablespoon vegetable oil
- 1 yellow or green bell pepper, diced
- 2 teaspoons bottled or fresh minced garlic
- 2 teaspoons bottled or fresh minced jalapeños
- ¼ cup canned chicken broth or picante sauce
- 1 large tomato, diced
- ¼ cups chopped cilantro
- 16 taco shells or small flour tortillas
- 2 cups (8 oz.) crumbled queso fresco cheese or shredded Mexican cheese
- Optional toppings: Salsa or picante sauce, shredded lettuce, sour cream, diced avocado or guacamole

Cut turkey into 1/2-inch chunks; toss with chili powder and salt. Heat oil in a large deep skillet over medium-high heat. Add turkey, bell pepper, garlic, ground cumin and jalapeños. Stir-fry 5 minutes or until turkey is no longer pink in center. Add broth; simmer uncovered 3 minutes, stirring occasionally. Stir in tomato and cilantro; heat through. Spoon mixture into taco shells; sprinkle with cheese and serve with toppings as desired.

Makes 8 servings.

Nutrition information per serving: Calories: 343, Protein: 28g, Carbohydrates: 24g, Fat: 16g, Cholesterol: 60mg, Sodium: 729mg

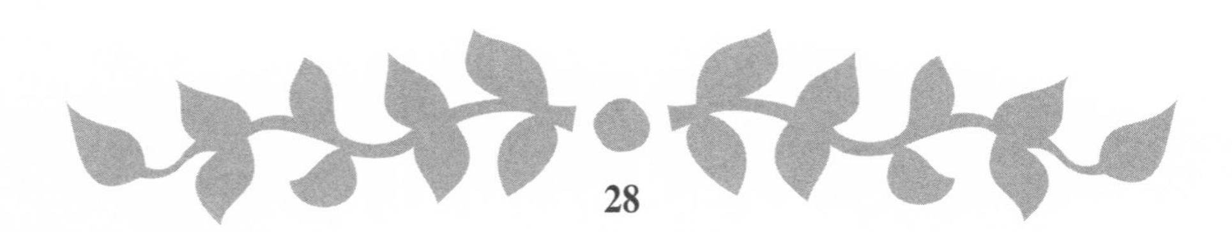

Quick & Easy Tacos

1 pkg. The Turkey Store® Lean Ground
1 tablespoon dried onion
1 tablespoon Mexican seasoning or 2 teaspoons chili powder plus 1 teaspoon ground cumin
2 teaspoons bottled or fresh minced garlic
¼ teaspoon salt
¾ cup picante sauce
12 taco shells
1-½ cups (6 oz.) shredded Mexican or cheddar cheese
Optional toppings: shredded lettuce, diced tomato, sour cream, guacamole or diced avocado, salsa, chopped cilantro

Crumble turkey into large nonstick skillet; add onion, seasoning, garlic and salt. Cook over medium-high heat 5 minutes, stirring occasionally. Add picante sauce; simmer 5 minutes. Spoon into taco shells; top with cheese. Serve with toppings as desired.

Makes 6 servings.

Nutrition information per serving: Calories: 349, Protein: 31g, Carbohydrates: 22g, Fat: 16g, Cholesterol: 71mg, Sodium: 722mg

LIGHT TANTALIZING TACOS

Cooking spray
1 medium onion, chopped
1 green bell pepper, chopped
3 cloves garlic, minced
1 pkg. The Turkey Store® Extra Lean Ground Breast
1 tablespoon chili powder
1 teaspoon ground cumin
¾ teaspoon salt (optional)
¾ cup prepared salsa
12 (7 inch) soft flour tortillas
1-½ cups (6 oz.) shredded low-fat cheddar cheese
1-½ cups shredded lettuce
1 cup chopped tomato
Optional toppings: fat-free or light sour cream, chopped cilantro, additional salsa

Coat a large nonstick skillet with cooking spray and place over medium-high heat. Add onion, green pepper and garlic; cook 4 minutes, stirring occasionally. Crumble turkey into skillet; sprinkle with chili powder, cumin and salt. Cook 5 minutes or until turkey is no longer pink, stirring frequently. Add salsa; simmer 10 to 12 minutes or until sauce thickens. Spoon 1/3 cup mixture onto each tortilla; top with cheese, lettuce and tomato. Serve with desired toppings.

Makes 6 servings.

Nutrition information per serving: Calories: 382, Protein: 37g, Carbohydrates: 38g, Fat: 10g, Cholesterol: 56mg, Sodium: 753mg

SLOPPY JOE RECIPES

Did You Know That?

Nobody knows when the Sloppy Joe made its debut or who really invented it. But one regional variation appeared as early as 1934 in Sioux City, Iowa at Ye Olde Tavern Inn, according to John Mariani in The Dictionary of American Food and Drink. It was called the "loose meat sandwich," the brainchild of Abraham and Bertha Kaled. The first printed Sloppy Joe recipe appeared in 1961. But we do know it has been an American favorite for more than 50 years.

Menu Makers

• Summer suppers: serve Traditional Sloppy Joes with pickles, potato salad or macaroni salad and coleslaw. Sliced tomatoes drizzled with Italian dressing and sprinkled with freshly chopped basil makes a great mealtime match for Italian Sloppy Joes. Spicy Sloppy Joes call for taco chips and ripe, green olives.

• Winter warmers: serve Traditional Sloppy Joes with vegetable soup and a side of Boston baked beans. For Italian Sloppy Joes, start with minestrone soup and present sandwiches with a serving of drained, pickled hot giardiniera vegetables (available in the Italian section of the supermarket). Spicy Sloppy Joes go nicely with corn chowder.

Tips and Tricks

• Some like it sloppy and eat their Sloppy Joes with their hands as they would any sandwich. Others are more fastidious. So provide a knife and fork and extra napkins to cover all bases.

• Keeping buns fresh: buns will stay moist and soft at room temperature for at least three days, unless they are French- or Italian-type bread made without shortening. These grow hard and dry within a day or two. All bread keeps better at room temperature or frozen than in the refrigerator. So if you plan to keep buns for some time, tightly double wrap and freeze. Let thaw, wrapped, at room temperature. Or remove plastic wrap; place buns or bread in brown paper bag well-sprinkled with water. Place bag in 350°F oven for 10 to 15 minutes. Re-warming bread in the microwave is tricky, because too long a time will make the bread tough.

• Sloppy not soggy: the longer they sit, the soggier they get. To prevent buns from getting soggy, assemble Sloppy Joes just before serving.

SLOPPY JOE
RECIPES

TRADITIONAL SLOPPY JOES

- 1 tablespoon vegetable oil
- 1 small onion, chopped
- ½ cup diced green or yellow bell pepper
- 3 cloves garlic, minced
- 1 pkg. The Turkey Store® Lean Ground
- 1 can (8 oz.) tomato sauce
- 2 tablespoons Worcestershire sauce
- 1 tablespoon tomato paste
- ¾ teaspoon salt
- ¼ teaspoon freshly ground black pepper
- 5 onion rolls or hamburger buns, split, toasted

Heat oil in a large skillet over medium heat. Add onion, bell pepper and garlic; cook 3 minutes, stirring occasionally. Crumble turkey into skillet; cook 3 minutes, stirring occasionally. Add tomato sauce, Worcestershire, tomato paste, salt and pepper. Simmer uncovered 10 to 15 minutes or until sauce thickens. Spoon mixture onto bottom of rolls; close with roll tops.

Makes 5 servings.

Nutrition information per serving: Calories: 390, Protein: 31g, Carbohydrates: 42g, Fat: 13g, Cholesterol: 70mg, Sodium: 1,078mg

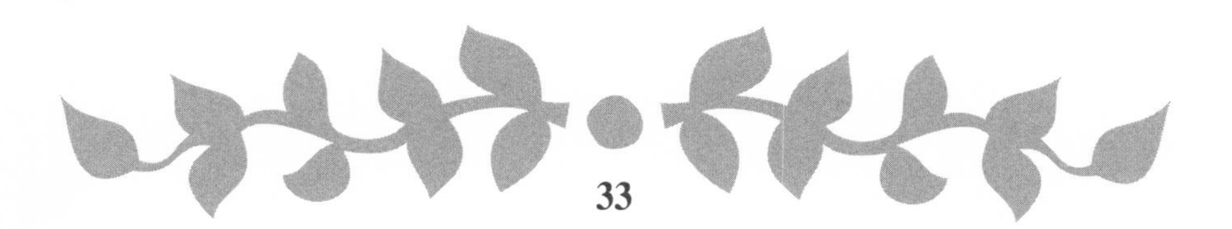

Spicy Sloppy Joes

- 1 tablespoon vegetable oil
- 1 small onion, chopped
- ½ cup diced green or yellow bell pepper
- 3 cloves garlic, minced
- 1 pkg. The Turkey Store® Lean Ground
- 1 cup chili sauce
- 2 tablespoons Worcestershire sauce
- 1 tablespoon tomato paste
- ½ teaspoon salt
- ½ teaspoon hot pepper sauce
- 5 onion rolls or hamburger buns, split, toasted

Heat oil in a large skillet over medium heat. Add onion, bell pepper and garlic; cook 3 minutes, stirring occasionally. Crumble turkey into skillet; cook 3 minutes, stirring occasionally. Add chili sauce, Worcestershire, tomato paste, salt and hot pepper sauce. Simmer uncovered 10 to 15 minutes or until sauce thickens. Spoon mixture onto bottom of rolls; close with roll tops.

Makes 5 servings.

Nutrition information per serving: Calories: 390, Protein: 36g, Carbohydrates: 52g, Fat: 6g, Cholesterol: 55mg, Sodium: 1,422mg

Italian Sausage Sloppy Joes

1 tablespoon olive oil
1 green or yellow bell pepper, chopped
2 teaspoons bottled or fresh minced garlic
1 pkg. The Turkey Store® Hot or Sweet Lean Italian Sausage
1 cup prepared spaghetti (see pg. 13) or marinara sauce
1 tablespoon chopped basil or 1 teaspoon dried basil
4 (6 to 8 inch) Italian or French bread rolls, split, toasted if desired.
½ cup (2 oz.) shredded mozzarella cheese

Heat oil in a large skillet over medium heat. Add bell pepper and garlic; cook 3 minutes, stirring occasionally. Crumble sausage into skillet, discarding casings. Cook 8 minutes or until no longer pink, stirring frequently. Add spaghetti sauce and basil; simmer uncovered 5 to 7 minutes or until thickened. Spoon mixture onto bottom of rolls; top with cheese and roll tops.
Makes 4 servings.

Nutrition information per serving: Calories: 457, Protein: 29g, Carbohydrates: 47g, Fat: 17g, Cholesterol: 64mg, Sodium: 1,519

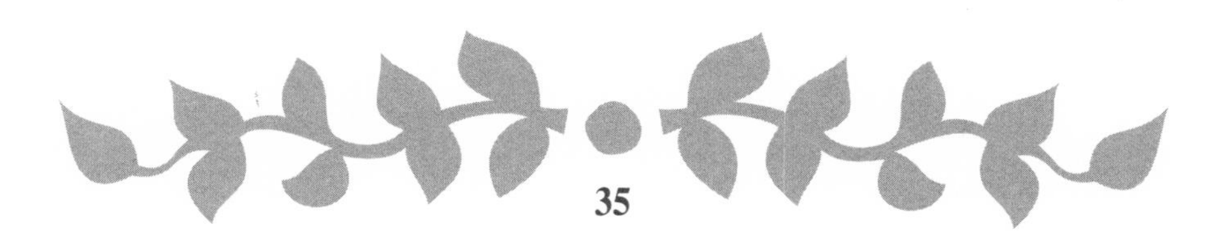

LIGHT SLOPPY JOES

Cooking spray
1 small onion, chopped
½ cup diced green or yellow bell pepper
3 cloves garlic, minced
1 pkg. The Turkey Store® Extra Lean Ground Breast
1 can (8 oz.) tomato sauce
2 tablespoons Worcestershire sauce
1 tablespoon tomato paste
¾ teaspoon salt (optional)
¼ teaspoon freshly ground black pepper
5 kaiser rolls, split, toasted

Coat a large nonstick skillet with cooking spray; place over medium heat. Add onion, bell pepper and garlic; cook 3 minutes, stirring occasionally. Crumble turkey into skillet; cook 3 minutes, stirring occasionally. Add tomato sauce, Worcestershire, tomato paste, salt and pepper. Simmer uncovered 10 to 15 minutes or until sauce thickens. Spoon mixture onto bottom of rolls; close with roll tops.
Makes 5 servings.

Nutrition information per serving: Calories: 293, Protein: 33g, Carbohydrates: 37g, Fat: 2g, Cholesterol: 55mg, Sodium: 735mg

FOOD FOR THOUGHT

SAUSAGE SANDWICH RECIPES

Did You Know That?

The art of sausage making is thousands of years old. In 48 B.C. Julius Caesar introduced sausage making to Rome. European settlers brought the idea to America, where more than 200 different varieties are now produced. Sausages are made from all kinds of meat, poultry and seafood, but all of them have one thing in common: spice.

Menu Makers

- Hearty sausage sandwiches are meals in themselves. But adding a simple skewered garnish will make the plate extra special. Disposable 6-inch wooden skewers are widely available.
- Garnish Smoky Spanish Sandwiches with a skewer of pimiento-stuffed green olives.
- Bratwurst & Grilled Onion Hoagies look and taste great with a skewer of bright red cherry tomatoes.
- For Smoked Sausage Sandwiches With Spicy Kraut, try threading two each of thinly sliced dill pickles and sweet bread-and-butter pickle slices on a wooden skewer.
- Garnish Sausage, Pepper & Onion Heroes with alternating slices of white mushrooms and green zucchini.

Tips and Tricks

- To reduce shrinkage, you may roll link sausages lightly in flour before frying. You may also put links in sauté pan and cover with cold water. Bring to boil, reduce heat and simmer for 5 minutes. Drain sausages and fry or grill as usual. You can also use these methods with sausage patties.
- Easy grilling: link sausages are easier to turn on the grill if you thread them on a long metal shish kabob skewer. After they are cooked on one side, simply lift and turn the skewer. Skewered sausages are easier to remove from the grill as well.
- Handling fresh chilies: when preparing fresh chilies, it's best to wear rubber or disposable plastic gloves. The capsaicin (the compound that gives chilies their heat) can cause a burning sensation on the skin that may last for hours. Never put hands near eyes when handling chilies. Most of the heat in chilies is in the seeds and white inner membranes. To reduce heat, scrape and discard seeds and membranes.
- The Scoville Scale: there are more than 200 different kinds of chilies with varying degrees of heat from mild to fiery. Heat in chilies is measured by the Scoville Scale from 0 to 10, named after Wilbur L. Scoville, a pharmacologist who invented it by having volunteers taste-test chilies. Bell peppers (green, red, yellow) are 0 on the Scoville Scale. Anaheims are 2-3; jalapeños are 5, and serranos are 6. The world's hottest pepper is the habanero, which ranks 10 on the Scoville Scale.

SAUSAGE
SANDWICH
RECIPES

SAUSAGE, PEPPER & ONION HEROES

- 2 tablespoons olive oil
- 1 green bell pepper
- 1 yellow or red bell pepper
- 4 slices (¼ inch) red or yellow onion, separated into rings
- 1 pkg. The Turkey Store® Sweet Lean Italian Sausage
- 5 hoagie or submarine sandwich rolls, split, toasted if desired
- ¾ cup prepared pizza or spaghetti sauce, heated

Prepare grill or preheat broiler. Cut bell peppers lengthwise into 1/4-inch strips. Heat 1 tablespoon oil in a large skillet over medium heat. Add pepper strips and onion rings; cook about 15 minutes or until vegetables are tender, stirring frequently. Sprinkle lightly with salt, if desired.

Meanwhile, brush remaining 1 tablespoon of the oil over sausages. Grill or broil about 5 inches from heat source 14 to 16 minutes or until lightly browned and no longer pink in center, turning occasionally. Serve sausages in rolls topped with pizza sauce and vegetables.

Makes 5 servings.

Nutrition information per serving: Calories: 398, Protein: 22g, Carbohydrates: 45g, Fat: 15g, Cholesterol: 45mg, Sodium: 1,159mg

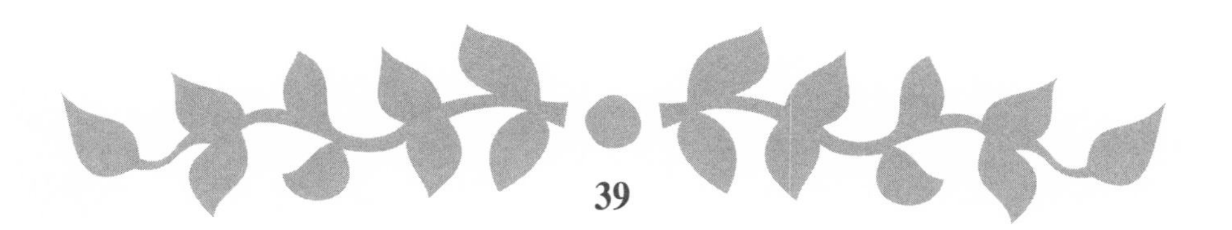

SMOKED SAUSAGE SANDWICHES WITH SPICY KRAUT TOPPING

1 pkg. The Turkey Store® Smoke Seasoned Lean Sausage

¾ cup well drained bottled sauerkraut

¼ cup drained pickled hot giardiniera vegetables

½ teaspoon caraway seeds (optional)

5 hoagie or submarine sandwich rolls, split, toasted if desired

Dijon or other prepared mustard (optional)

Cook sausages according to package directions. Meanwhile, combine sauerkraut, pickled vegetables and caraway seeds, if using; mix well. Serve sausages in rolls topped with sauerkraut mixture. Serve with mustard, if desired.

Makes 5 servings.

Nutrition information per serving: Calories: 325, Protein: 21g, Carbohydrates: 38g, Fat: 10g, Cholesterol: 65mg, Sodium: 1,232mg

BRATWURST & GRILLED ONION HOAGIES

- 1 tablespoon butter or margarine
- 1 large onion, thinly sliced, separated into rings
- ½ teaspoon paprika
- ¼ teaspoon salt
- ¼ teaspoon freshly ground black pepper
- 1 pkg. The Turkey Store® Lean Bratwurst
- ½ cup beer (option: non-alcoholic beer or water)
- 2 teaspoons olive or vegetable oil
- 5 hoagie or submarine sandwich rolls, split, lightly toasted
- Spicy brown mustard (optional)

Melt butter in a large skillet over medium-high heat. Add onion rings; cook 3 minutes or until wilted, stirring occasionally. Sprinkle with paprika, salt and pepper. Reduce heat to medium-low; cook 15 to 20 minutes or until golden brown and tender, stirring occasionally.

Meanwhile, combine bratwurst and either beer or water in a large saucepan. Cover and simmer 10 minutes. Pour off and discard liquid. Add oil to pan; brown bratwurst on all sides, about 6 minutes. Serve in rolls topped with onions, and, if desired, mustard. Makes 5 servings.

Nutrition information per serving: Calories: 378, Protein: 22g, Carbohydrates: 43g, Fat: 13g, Cholesterol: 51mg, Sodium: 1,049

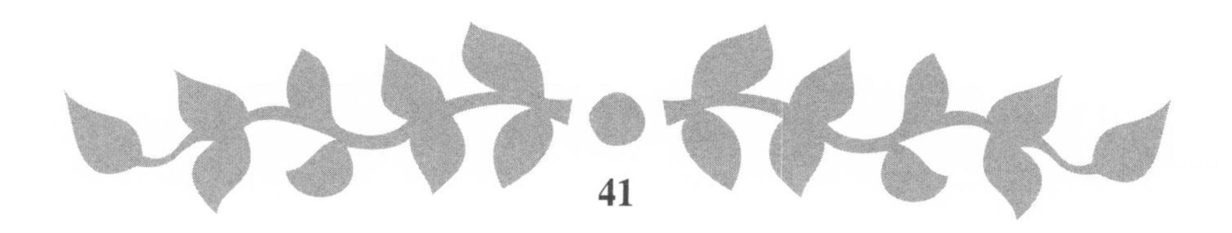

SMOKY SPANISH SANDWICHES

- 1 tablespoon olive oil
- ½ cup chopped onion
- 2 teaspoons bottled or fresh minced garlic
- 2 teaspoons minced, seeded jalapeño or serrano chilies
- 1-½ cups diced tomato
- 2 tablespoons tomato paste
- 2 tablespoons drained bottled capers
- 1 teaspoon dried oregano
- ¼ teaspoon sugar
- 1 pkg. The Turkey Store® Smoke Seasoned Lean Sausage
- 5 hoagie or submarine sandwich rolls, split, lightly toasted

Heat oil in a medium saucepan over medium-high heat. Add onion, garlic and minced chilies; cook 5 minutes, stirring occasionally. Add tomato, tomato paste, capers, oregano and sugar. Simmer 5 minutes. Grill or broil sausages according to package directions. Serve sausages in rolls topped with tomato mixture.
Makes 5 servings.

Nutrition information per serving: Calories: 377, Protein: 23g, Carbohydrates: 43g, Fat: 13g, Cholesterol: 72mg, Sodium: 1,125mg

FOOD FOR THOUGHT

CHILI RECIPES

Did You Know That?

Chili is short for chili con carne, a dish created in Texas. Chili has been written about since 1828. The dish is referred to as a "Bowl of Red," from a book by that name by the late Frank X. Tolbert, Texas restaurateur and founder of the International Chili Appreciation Society. The society still holds an annual world championship chili cookoff in Terlingua, Texas to this day. When it comes to controversy, chili is champion. Texans think that adding beans to their original dish of meat and chili peppers is a crime. In other states, chili isn't chili without the beans. Some recipes call for chopped meat, others for ground meat. Every region has its own version, the most famous of which is the Cincinnati five-way chili: spaghetti topped with chili, chopped onions, red kidney beans, and shredded cheese. Today's popular chili powder was first created by English settlers in 1828 in what was then Mexico's Texas Territory as a quick-and-easy way to season local Mexican-style dishes. The first commercial chili powder was manufactured by a German-American cafe owner named William Gebhardt in New Braunfels, Texas, in 1894.

Menu Makers

• Chili lends itself to dozens of delicious side dishes; among them, cornbread is probably king. For easy corn bread, add any of the following to packaged corn bread mix: canned, drained corn kernels; grated cheddar or Monterey jack cheese; canned, diced mild green chilies; bacon bits; chopped green onions. Bake batter in a square or round cake pan and cut into wedges or squares. Or else make corn muffins.

• For a complete meal, add some green to your Bowl of Red with a big green salad mixed with grapefruit segments, thinly sliced red onions and topped with chopped almonds.

Tips and Tricks

• Chipotle chilies are smoked dried jalapeño peppers. Canned chipotle chilies in adobo sauce are widely available in the Hispanic foods section of supermarkets. The chilies in the tomato-based sauce are usually whole, so to reduce heat, slice open chilies, scrape out seeds and membranes, then chop chilies and add back into the sauce.

• Leftover chipotles? Puree chilies and sauce in food processor or blender, then scrape puree with rubber spatula into ice cube trays. Freeze; store frozen cubes in plastic bags in freezer for later use in soups, stews, tacos and other Southwestern favorites.

CHILI
RECIPES

TEX-MEX CHILI

1 tablespoon vegetable oil
1 medium onion, chopped
3 cloves garlic, minced
1 pkg. The Turkey Store® Lean Ground
1 tablespoon chili powder
1 tablespoon ground cumin
¾ teaspoon salt
2 cans (14-½ oz.) salsa-style or regular stewed tomatoes, undrained
1 can (16 oz.) kidney or pinto beans, drained
1 green bell pepper, diced
¾ cup picante sauce or salsa
Optional toppings: shredded cheddar or Monterey jack cheese, sour cream, chopped cilantro

Heat oil in a large saucepan over medium heat. Add onion and garlic; cook 5 minutes, stirring occasionally. Crumble turkey into saucepan; sprinkle with chili powder, cumin and salt. Cook 5 minutes, stirring occasionally. Add tomatoes, beans, bell pepper and picante sauce. Bring to a boil over high heat. Reduce heat; simmer uncovered 10 minutes, stirring occasionally. Ladle into bowls; top as desired.
Makes 6 servings.

Nutrition information per serving: Calories: 282, Protein: 26g, Carbohydrates: 28g, Fat: 10g, Cholesterol: 58mg, Sodium: 1,040mg

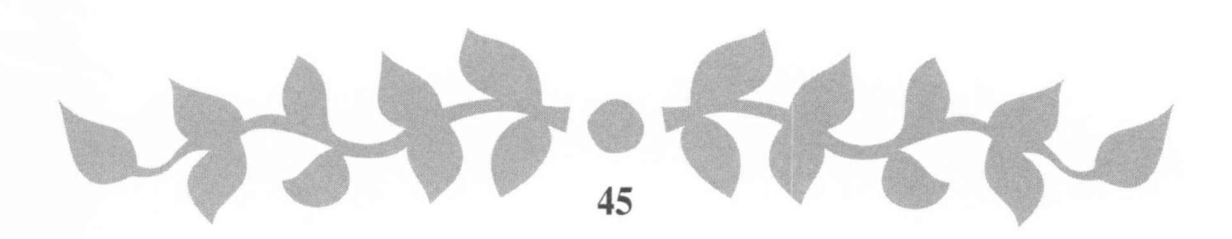

SMOKY CHIPOTLE CHILI

CHILI RECIPES

- 1 tablespoon vegetable oil
- 1 cup coarsely chopped onion
- 2 poblano or banana chilies, coarsely chopped
- ½ cup coarsely chopped red or yellow bell pepper
- 2 teaspoons bottled or fresh minced garlic
- 1 can (14-½ oz.) chili-style or salsa-style diced tomatoes, undrained
- 1 can (13-¾ oz.) beef broth
- 2 to 3 tablespoons chopped canned chipotle chilies in adobo sauce, as desired
- 1 pkg. The Turkey Store® Smoke Seasoned Lean Sausage
- 2 teaspoons chili powder
- 1 can (16 oz.) black beans or red beans, rinsed and drained
- Optional toppings: sour cream, shredded cheddar or Mexican cheese, chopped cilantro

Heat oil in a large saucepan over medium heat. Add onion, chili peppers, bell pepper and garlic. Cook 5 minutes, stirring occasionally. Crumble sausage into saucepan; discard casings. Cook 5 minutes, breaking sausage into chunks and stirring occasionally. Add tomatoes, broth, chipotle chilies and chili powder; bring to a simmer. Simmer uncovered 10 minutes. Stir beans into chili; continue to simmer 5 minutes. Ladle into bowls; serve with toppings as desired.

Makes 6 servings.

Nutrition information per serving: Calories: 250, Protein: 18g, Carbohydrates: 21g, Fat: 11g, Cholesterol: 54mg, Sodium: 1,291mg

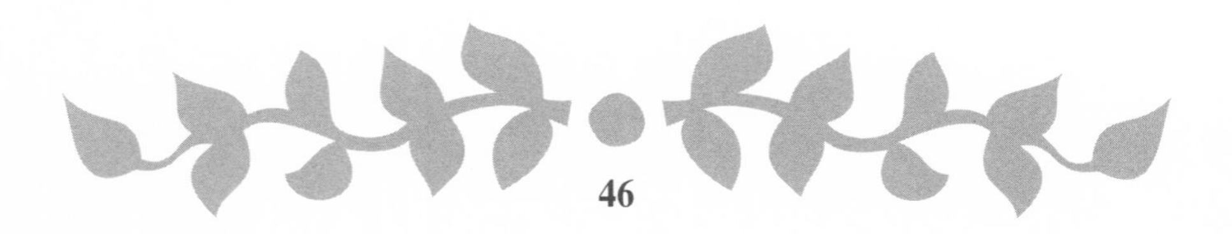

QUICK & EASY CHILI

1 pkg. The Turkey Store® Lean Ground
1 tablespoon chili powder
1 tablespoon dried onion
2 teaspoons bottled minced garlic
2 cans (15-½ oz.) chili beans in spicy sauce, undrained
1 can (14-½ oz.) salsa-style or chili-style tomatoes, undrained
Optional toppings: shredded cheddar cheese, sour cream, chopped cilantro

Crumble turkey into a large saucepan; add chili powder, onion and garlic. Cook over medium-high heat 5 minutes, stirring occasionally. Add beans and tomatoes; bring to a simmer. Simmer uncovered 10 minutes, stirring occasionally. Serve with desired toppings.
Makes 6 servings.

Nutrition information per serving: Calories: 228, Protein: 31g, Carbohydrates: 29g, Fat: 3g, Cholesterol: 46mg, Sodium: 862mg

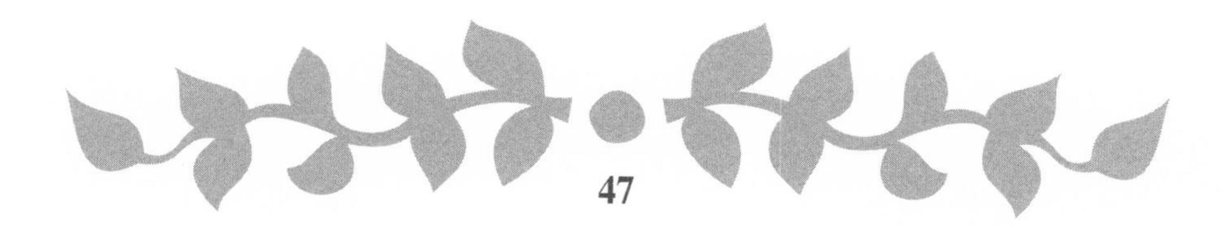

Light Tex-Mex Chili

- Cooking spray
- 1 medium onion, chopped
- 3 cloves garlic, minced
- 1 pkg. The Turkey Store® Extra Lean Ground Breast
- 1 tablespoon chili powder
- 1 tablespoon ground cumin
- ¾ teaspoon salt (optional)
- 2 cans (14-½ oz.) salsa-style or regular stewed tomatoes, undrained
- 1 can (16 oz.) kidney or pinto beans, drained
- 1 green bell pepper, diced
- ¾ cup picante sauce or salsa
- Optional toppings: shredded low-fat cheddar cheese, nonfat or light sour cream, chopped cilantro

Coat a large saucepan with cooking spray. Add onion and garlic; cook over medium heat 5 minutes, stirring occasionally. Crumble turkey into saucepan; sprinkle with chili powder, cumin and salt. Cook 5 minutes, stirring occasionally. Add tomatoes, beans, bell pepper and picante sauce. Bring to a boil over high heat. Reduce heat; simmer uncovered 10 minutes, stirring occasionally. Serve with desired toppings.

Makes 6 servings.

Nutrition information per serving: Calories: 228, Protein: 29g, Carbohydrates: 28g, Fat: 3g, Cholesterol: 46mg, Sodium: 769mg

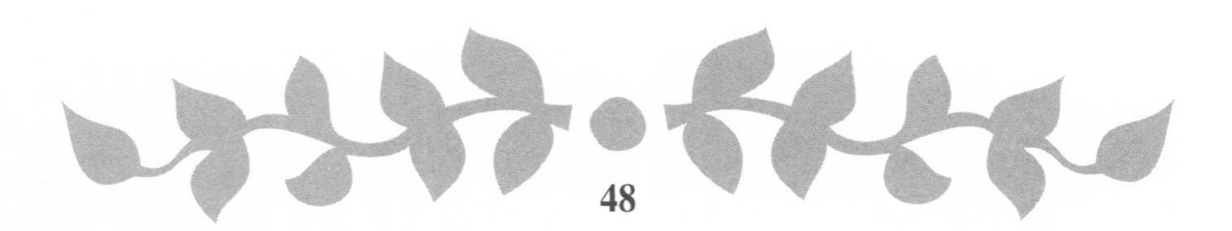

SOUP RECIPES

Did You Know That?

In the book Why We Eat What We Eat, food historian Raymond Sokolov suggests that our familiar word "soup" comes from "sop," or a piece of bread left in liquid to soften. The phrase "Soup Kitchen" dates from 1851 and was a military term used to describe the Mess. During the Great Depression (1929-1934), it took on another meaning: the kitchen of a charitable group which passed out soup and bread to the unemployed. Soup can be dry as well: As early as 1733, boiled down, dried broth tablets, carried by travelers in their pockets were known as "pocket soup." Instant dehydrated soup has been manufactured in America since 1883, and condensed soup has been around since 1897.

Menu Makers

- Soup and salad are modern menu classics. Along with bread, they make a complete meal. And, each meal is different every time you vary the bread, salad and soup.
- Try Tuscan Bean & Tomato Soup with a green salad and a large loaf of crusty Italian bread, garlic bread or hearth-baked olive bread.
- Sausage & Rice Soup is a nice match with tangy caraway-rye bread and Caesar salad.
- Turkey Noodle Soup and whole wheat bread are naturals. Try it with an old-fashioned wedge of iceberg lettuce dressed with Thousand Island or French dressing.
- Marvelous Mushroom Barley Soup—with its European flavors—stands up to a hearty, dark pumpernickel bread and coleslaw or crisp Waldorf salad.
- Serve Creamy Corn Chowder with biscuits hot from the oven and a salad of sliced red tomatoes.

Tips and Tricks

- The shape of your pot affects the way soup cooks. A wide pot with low sides allows the liquid to evaporate rapidly. A narrow stock pot with high sides lets the soup cook without excess evaporation.
- Always taste soup for seasoning before serving; add salt and pepper if needed.
- Soup left to simmer continues to reduce—that is, the water evaporates and the soup becomes thicker. It may also become much saltier, so before serving soup that has been simmering, taste for salt. Dilute soup as needed with water.
- If you have time, make soups a day ahead and refrigerate. This allows any excess fat to rise to the surface and solidify where it can be easily removed before reheating. Overnight refrigeration also allows the flavors to mellow and blend.

SOUP
RECIPES

TUSCAN BEAN & TOMATO SOUP

- 2 tablespoons rosemary-infused or extra virgin olive oil
- ½ cup sliced shallots or chopped sweet onion
- 3 cloves garlic, minced
- 1 pkg. The Turkey Store® Hot or Sweet Lean Italian Sausage
- 2 cans (16 oz.) great northern beans, rinsed, drained
- 1 can (14-½ oz.) pasta-style seasoned tomatoes or diced tomatoes, undrained
- 1 can (13-¾ oz.) reduced sodium chicken broth
- ¾ teaspoon dried rosemary, crushed
- ¼ teaspoon freshly ground black pepper
- ½ cup garlic or herb croutons

SOUP RECIPES

Heat 1 tablespoon oil in a large saucepan over medium heat. Add shallots and garlic; cook 5 minutes, stirring occasionally. Meanwhile, cut sausage into 1/2-inch slices; remove and discard casings. Add sausage to saucepan; cook 5 minutes, stirring occasionally. Add beans, tomatoes, broth, rosemary and pepper; bring to a boil over high heat. Reduce heat; simmer uncovered 15 minutes or until sausage is no longer pink in center. Stir in remaining 1 tablespoon oil. Ladle into shallow bowls; top with croutons.

Makes 6 servings.

Nutrition information per serving: Calories: 331, Protein: 19g, Carbohydrates: 34g, Fat: 13g, Cholesterol: 39mg, Sodium: 1,280mg

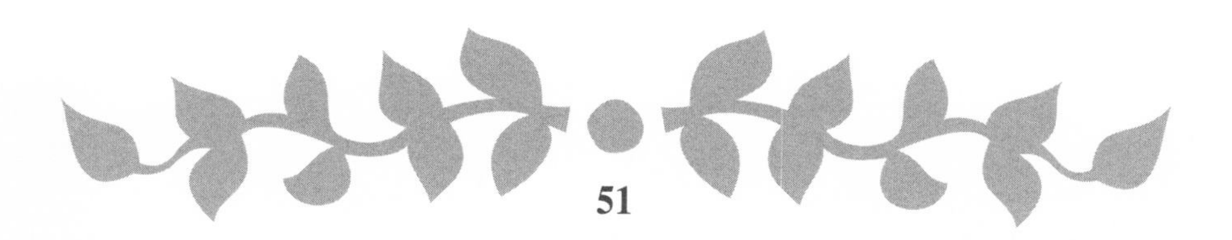

Turkey Noodle Soup

- 2 tablespoons butter or margarine
- 2 carrots, thinly sliced
- 1 medium onion, chopped
- ½ cup thinly sliced celery
- 1 large can (48 oz.) chicken broth
- 2 cups (4 oz.) thin egg noodles, uncooked
- 1 pkg. The Turkey Store® Breast Strips
- ½ teaspoon salt
- ¼ teaspoon freshly ground black pepper
- ¼ cup chopped parsley or celery leaves

Melt 1 tablespoon butter in a large saucepan over medium-high heat. Add carrots, onion and celery; cook 1 minute. Reduce heat; cover and cook 8 minutes. Add broth and noodles; bring to a boil over high heat. Reduce heat; simmer uncovered 10 minutes or until noodles are tender. Meanwhile, melt remaining 1 tablespoon butter in a large skillet. Add turkey; cook 3 to 4 minutes or until no longer pink, stirring frequently. Sprinkle with salt and pepper; add to soup and heat through. Stir in parsley. *Makes 6 servings.*

Nutrition information per serving: Calories: 247, Protein: 24g, Carbohydrates: 17g, Fat: 10g, Cholesterol: 70mg, Sodium: 1,259mg

MARVELOUS MUSHROOM BARLEY SOUP

- ½ oz. dried mushrooms, preferably porcini
- 1 cup boiling water
- 2 tablespoons butter or margarine
- 1 pkg. (8 oz.) sliced mushrooms or 2 pkg. (4 oz.) sliced exotic mushrooms
- ½ cup chopped shallots or onion
- 2 cloves garlic, minced
- 2 cans (13-¾ oz.) beef broth
- ½ cup quick-cooking pearl barley
- 1 tablespoon chopped fresh thyme or 1 teaspoon dried thyme
- 1 pkg. The Turkey Store® Breast Strips
- 1 teaspoon paprika
- ½ teaspoon freshly ground black pepper
- ¼ teaspoon salt

Soak dried mushrooms in boiling water 20 minutes or until softened. Meanwhile, melt 1 tablespoon butter in a large saucepan over medium-high heat. Add sliced mushrooms, shallots and garlic; cook 8 minutes, stirring occasionally. Drain soaked mushrooms, reserving liquid. Coarsely chop mushrooms. Add chopped mushrooms, broth, barley, thyme and mushroom soaking liquid to saucepan; bring to a boil. Reduce heat; cover and simmer 15 to 18 minutes, or until barley is tender. Meanwhile, toss turkey strips with paprika, pepper and salt. Melt remaining 1 tablespoon butter in a large skillet over medium-high heat. Add turkey; stir-fry 2 to 3 minutes or until lightly browned. Stir into soup; heat through.
Makes 6 servings.

Nutrition information per serving: Calories: 209, Protein: 26g, Carbohydrates: 15g, Fat: 5g, Cholesterol: 50mg, Sodium: 743mg

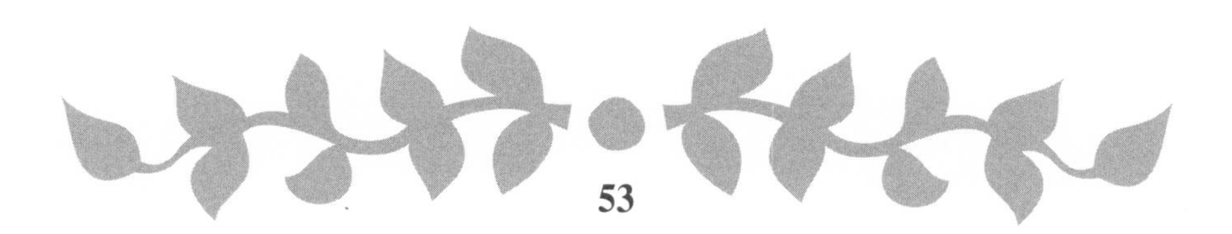

SAUSAGE & RICE SOUP

- 2 tablespoons butter or margarine
- 1 large or 2 medium leeks, white and light green parts sliced
- 2 carrots, thinly sliced
- 1 pkg. The Turkey Store® Lean Polish Sausage
- 2 cups diced mixed bell peppers, preferably red and yellow
- 2 cans (13-¾ oz.) reduced sodium chicken broth
- 1 cup water
- ¾ cup quick-cooking brown rice, uncooked
- ½ teaspoon dried sage
- ¼ teaspoon freshly ground black pepper
- Chopped fresh chives (optional)

SOUP RECIPES

Melt butter in a large saucepan over medium heat. Add leeks and carrots; cook 5 minutes, stirring occasionally. Meanwhile, cut sausage into 1/2-inch slices; remove and discard casings. Add sausage to saucepan; cook 5 minutes, stirring occasionally. Add bell peppers, broth, water, rice, sage and pepper; bring to a boil over high heat. Reduce heat; simmer uncovered 15 minutes or until sausage is no longer pink in center and rice is tender. Ladle into bowls; top with chives, if desired.

Makes 6 servings.

Nutrition information per serving: Calories: 229, Protein: 14g, Carbohydrates: 18g, Fat: 12g, Cholesterol: 50mg, Sodium: 961mg

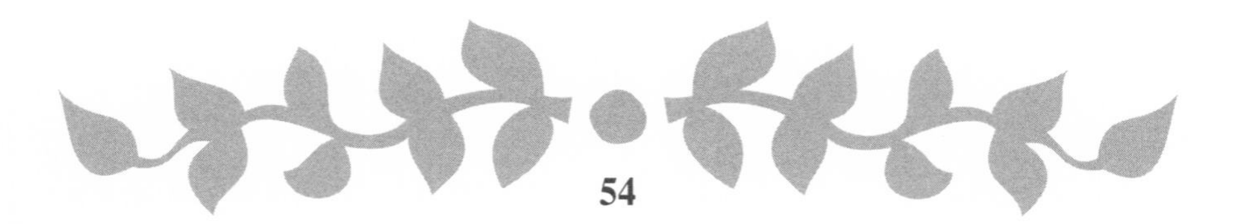

COMFORTING DOUBLE CORN CHOWDER

- 1 pkg. The Turkey Store® Lean Bratwurst or Smoke Seasoned Lean Sausage
- 1 cup chopped onion
- 1 can (15 oz.) cream-style corn
- 2 cups half-and-half or whole milk
- 1 cup fresh or frozen corn kernels
- ½ cup finely diced red or green bell pepper
- ¼ teaspoon freshly ground black pepper
- ¼ teaspoon hot pepper sauce
- ½ cup seasoned croutons
- Chopped chives or green onion tops (optional)

SOUP RECIPES

Crumble bratwurst into a large saucepan; discard casings. Add onion; cook over medium heat 8 minutes, breaking up bratwurst into chunks. Add creamed corn, half-and-half, corn kernels, bell pepper, black pepper and hot pepper sauce. Simmer uncovered 15 minutes, stirring occasionally. Ladle into soup bowls; top with croutons and chives, if desired.

Makes 6 servings.

Nutrition information per serving: Calories: 323, Protein: 17g, Carbohydrates: 29g, Fat: 17g, Cholesterol: 67mg, Sodium: 712mg

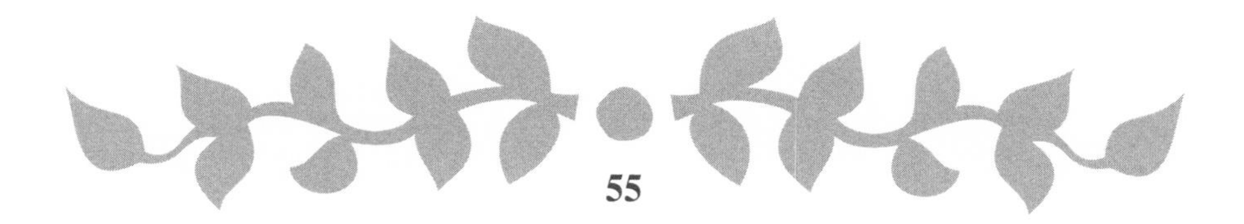

Light Comforting Double Corn Chowder

- 1 pkg. The Turkey Store® Lean Bratwurst or Smoke Seasoned Lean Sausage
- 1 cup chopped onion
- 1 tablespoon all-purpose flour
- 1 can (15 oz.) cream-style corn
- 1 cup fresh or frozen corn kernels
- 2 cups skim milk
- ½ cup finely diced red or green bell pepper
- ¼ teaspoon freshly ground black pepper
- ¼ teaspoon hot pepper sauce
- ½ cup seasoned croutons (optional)
- Chopped chives or green onion tops (optional)

Crumble bratwurst into a large saucepan; discard casings. Add onion; cook over medium heat 8 minutes, breaking up bratwurst into chunks. Sprinkle with flour; cook 1 minute, stirring constantly. Add creamed corn, corn kernels, milk, bell pepper, black pepper and hot pepper sauce. Simmer uncovered 15 minutes, stirring occasionally. Ladle into bowls; top with croutons and chives if desired.

Makes 6 servings.

Nutrition information per serving: Calories: 235, Protein: 17g, Carbohydrates: 28g, Fat: 7g, Cholesterol: 39mg, Sodium: 680mg

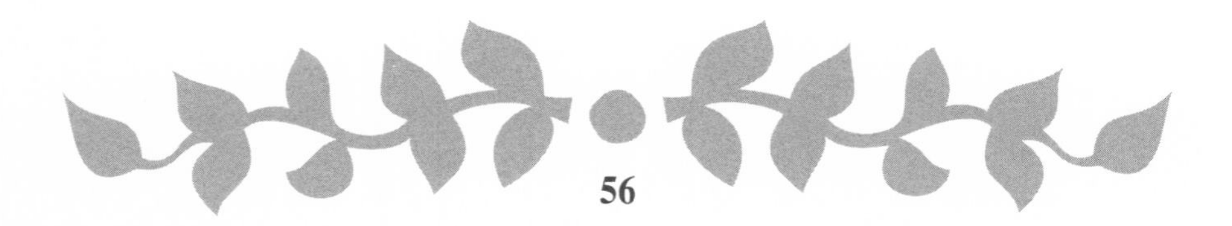

FOOD FOR THOUGHT

CAJUN RECIPES

Did You Know That?

The word Cajun started out as Acadian, after the French Acadians who settled in Acadia, Nova Scotia. They were forced to leave by the British in 1755 because they refused to swear allegiance to England. They migrated to Louisiana and were first called Cadians, then Cagians, and finally Cajuns. They were fishers, hunters and farmers, and developed a distinctive style of cooking known for its hot, spicy flavorings. They also created some famous dishes: jambalaya, etoufee and gumbo. Their lusty food was matched by their lust for life, expressed in their motto "Laissez le bon temps rouler," or, "Let the good times roll." Cajun cookery was first made famous by Louisiana Cajun Chef Paul Prudhomme, in his New Orleans restaurant K-Paul's Louisiana Kitchen, which opened in 1979.

Menu Makers

- New Orleans Gumbo has the traditional Cajun "trinity" of ingredients: green pepper, celery and onion. This hearty, smoky dish can be paired with crunchy corn on the cob or corn kernels and simply prepared fresh seasonal vegetable: carrots, peas, green beans or zucchini.
- Jambalaya—a mouthwatering combination of sausage and shrimp—calls for hot cornbread with a spinach and mushroom salad.
- Red Beans & Rice is a traditional Monday (washday) lunch in New Orleans because it "cooked by itself" while the laundry was being done. A meal in itself, it is good any day of the week for lunch and dinner. Keep it simple and serve it with a loaf of French bread and a green salad or a cooling scoop of coleslaw.

Tips and Tricks

- Filé (pronounced fee-lay) powder is the dried, ground leaves of the sassafras tree, first used by the Native American Choctaws in Louisiana. It was soon adopted into Cajun and Creole cookery to flavor and thicken stews. Filé powder is available in the spice section of supermarkets. It must be added after the dish has been removed from the heat; otherwise it will become tough and stringy.
- Cajun seasoning mixes are widely available in supermarkets. Each brand has its own special spice blend. Common spices include black, white and cayenne pepper, garlic and onion powder, thyme and mustard. All are hot and spicy.
- Blackened spice mixes are Cajun seasoning mixes usually rubbed onto meat, poultry or fish before frying in a cast iron skillet over exceedingly high heat, a technique popularized first in 1979 by Cajun Chef Paul Prudhomme.
- Creole seasoning mixes are usually somewhat milder than Cajun or blackened seasonings.

CAJUN
RECIPES

SMOKY JAMBALAYA

- 2 tablespoons olive oil
- 1 medium onion, chopped
- ½ cup thinly sliced celery
- 4 cloves garlic, minced
- 1 pkg. The Turkey Store® Smoke Seasoned Lean Sausage
- 2 cans (14-½ oz.) Cajun-style or regular stewed tomatoes, undrained
- 1 cup canned beef broth
- 1 bay leaf
- ¾ teaspoon dried thyme
- ¾ teaspoon hot sauce, plus additional for serving
- 8 ounces peeled and deveined large shrimp, thawed if frozen
- 3 cups hot cooked white rice
- ¼ cup chopped parsley

Heat oil in a large saucepan over medium heat. Add onion, celery and garlic; cook 5 minutes, stirring occasionally. Meanwhile, cut sausage into 3/4-inch pieces; remove and discard casings. Add to saucepan; cook 5 minutes, stirring occasionally. Add tomatoes, broth, bay leaf, thyme and hot sauce; bring to a boil. Simmer uncovered 15 minutes, stirring occasionally. Stir in shrimp; simmer 5 minutes or until shrimp are opaque. Ladle into shallow bowls; top each serving with 1/2 cup rice and sprinkle with parsley.
Makes 6 servings.

Nutrition information per serving: Calories: 355 Protein: 22g Carbohydrates: 37g Fat: 13g Cholesterol: 108mg Sodium: 1,016mg

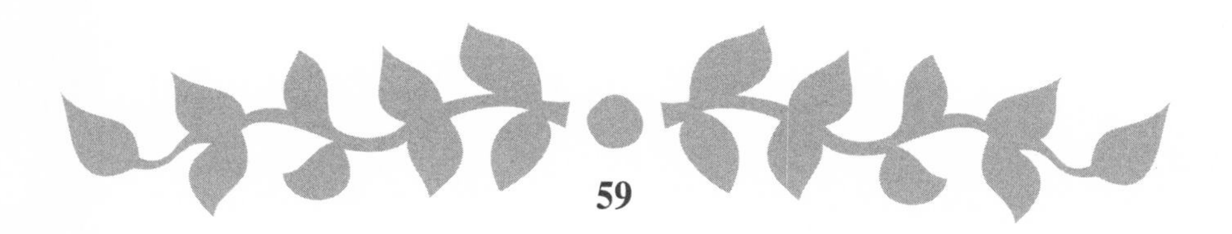

NEW ORLEANS GUMBO

CAJUN RECIPES

- 4 slices smoked bacon, thinly sliced crosswise
- 1 tablespoon olive oil
- 1 cup chopped onion
- 1 green bell pepper, chopped
- ¾ cup sliced celery
- 4 cloves garlic, minced
- 2 tablespoons all-purpose flour
- 1 tablespoon Cajun, blackened or Creole seasoning mix
- 1 pkg. The Turkey Store® Boneless Breast Tenderloins
- 1 can (14-½ oz.) Cajun-style or regular stewed tomatoes, undrained
- 1 can (13-¾ oz.) chicken broth
- 1 pkg. (10 oz.) frozen sliced okra, thawed
- ¼ teaspoon hot pepper sauce
- 1 teaspoon filé powder (optional)
- ¼ cup chopped parsley

Cook bacon in a large saucepan over medium heat until crisp. With slotted spoon, transfer bacon to paper towel; set aside. Add oil to same saucepan. Add onion, bell pepper, celery and garlic; cook 8 minutes, stirring occasionally. Combine flour and seasoning mix in plastic or paper bag. Cut turkey into 1-inch chunks; add to bag and toss to coat. Add turkey and any remaining flour mixture from bag to saucepan; cook 5 minutes, stirring occasionally. Add tomatoes, broth, okra and hot sauce; bring to a simmer. Simmer uncovered 12 to 15 minutes or until turkey is no longer pink in center and mixture thickens, stirring occasionally. Remove from heat; if desired, stir in filé powder. Ladle into bowls; top with parsley.

Makes 6 servings.

Nutrition information per serving: Calories: 269, Protein: 32g, Carbohydrates: 16g, Fat: 10g, Cholesterol: 60mg, Sodium: 952mg

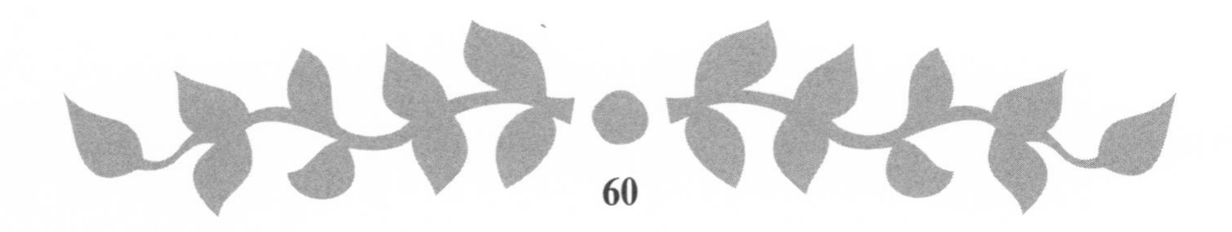

RED BEANS & RICE

- 1 tablespoon vegetable oil
- 1 cup chopped onion
- 1 green bell pepper, chopped
- ½ cup sliced celery
- 2 teaspoons bottled or fresh minced garlic
- 1 pkg. The Turkey Store® Lean Ground
- 1-½ teaspoons dried thyme
- 1 teaspoon hot pepper sauce
- ½ teaspoon salt
- 1 can (14-½ oz.) Cajun-style stewed tomatoes
- 1 can (16 oz.) red beans, rinsed and drained
- ¼ cup tomato paste
- 4 cups hot cooked white or brown rice
- ¼ cup chopped parsley

Heat oil in a large deep skillet over medium-high heat. Add onion, bell pepper, celery and garlic; cook 5 minutes, stirring occasionally. Crumble turkey into skillet; sprinkle with thyme, hot pepper sauce and salt. Cook 5 minutes, stirring occasionally. Add tomatoes, beans and tomato paste; simmer uncovered 10 minutes, stirring occasionally. Serve over rice; sprinkle with parsley and serve with additional hot sauce. *Makes 6 servings.*

Nutrition information per serving: Calories: 412, Protein: 31g, Carbohydrates: 62g, Fat: 4g, Cholesterol: 46mg, Sodium: 791mg

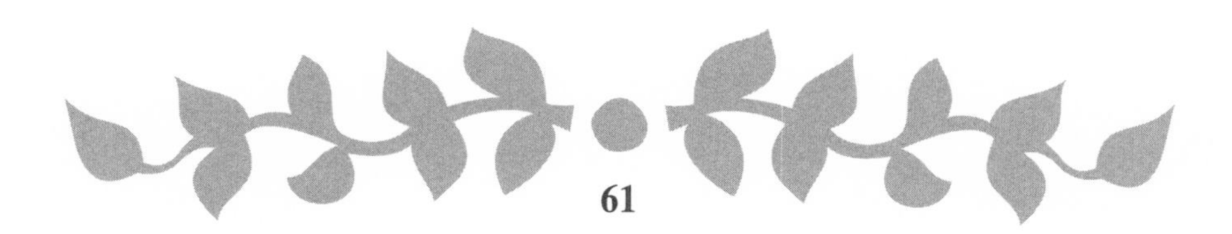

Light New Orleans Gumbo

- Cooking spray
- 1 cup chopped onion
- 1 green bell pepper, chopped
- ¾ cup sliced celery
- 4 cloves garlic, minced
- 2 tablespoons all-purpose flour
- 1 tablespoon Cajun, blackened or Creole seasoning mix
- 1 pkg. The Turkey Store® Boneless Breast Tenderloins
- 1 can (14-½ oz.) Cajun-style or regular stewed tomatoes, undrained
- 1 can (14-½ oz.) fat free, reduced sodium chicken broth
- 1 pkg. (10 oz.) frozen sliced okra, thawed
- ¼ teaspoon hot pepper sauce
- ¼ cup no saturated fat bacon bits
- 1 teaspoon filé powder (optional)
- ¼ cup chopped parsley

Coat a large nonstick saucepan or deep skillet with cooking spray; heat over medium heat. Add onion, bell pepper, celery and garlic; cook 8 minutes, stirring occasionally. Meanwhile, combine flour and seasoning mix in plastic or paper bag. Cut turkey into 1-inch chunks; add to bag and toss to coat. Add turkey and any remaining flour mixture from bag to saucepan; cook 5 minutes, stirring occasionally. Add tomatoes, broth, okra and hot sauce; bring to a simmer. Simmer uncovered 12 to 15 minutes or until turkey is no longer pink in center and mixture thickens, stirring occasionally. Remove from heat; stir in bacon bits and, if desired, filé powder. Ladle into bowls; top with parsley.

Makes 6 servings.

Nutrition information per serving: Calories: 203, Protein: 31g, Carbohydrates: 17g, Fat: 2g, Cholesterol: 53mg, Sodium: 785mg

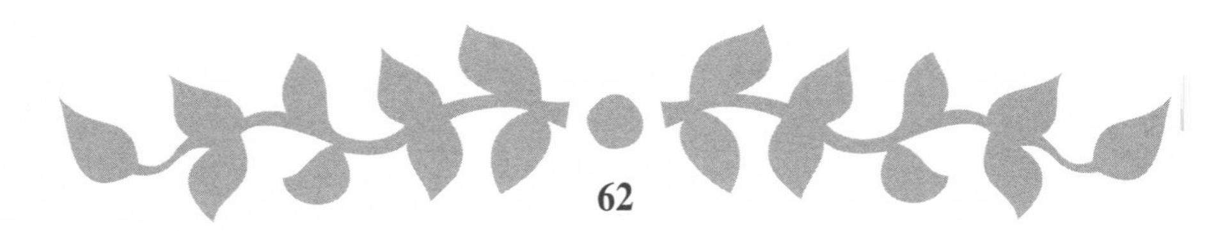

FOOD FOR THOUGHT

LASAGNA RECIPES

Did You Know That?

All good-quality dried pasta is made from hard, durum wheat which, unlike soft wheat, keeps its texture and shape during cooking. One of the very first pastas ever made from durum wheat was lasagna, according to Clifford A. Wright in Lasagne, his all-lasagna cookbook. (In Italian, lasagna is singular; lasagne is plural.) The first lasagna recipe appeared in print in the 14th century.

Menu Makers

• Lasagna and a big, green salad—who could ask for anything more? Well, for starters, you could ask for some interesting greens, such as a mixture of romaine lettuce, curly endive and chopped radicchio. Try adding a teaspoon or two of freshly chopped basil to a green salad.
• You might want to add some variety in salad dressings. In addition to Italian dressing and garlic vinaigrettes, prepared salad dressings made with red wine and balsamic vinegars are becoming easier to find.
• For that special touch, add a loaf of hot garlic bread and a dish of black olives.

Tips and Tricks

• There are two kinds of commercial dried lasagna: regular and no-boil or instant. Regular lasagna noodles need to be precooked before layering and baking; no-boil or instant lasagna can be layered and baked, covered, without first being boiled. No-boil lasagna noodles are thinner and look more translucent when held up to the light. Most brands are imported, but there is at least one American-made no-boil lasagna.
• If you find ricotta cheese hard to spread, try thinning it by mixing it with 5 or 6 tablespoons of milk.
• For easier cleanup, set your cooking pan on a metal baking tray in case the lasagna bubbles over its pan during baking.
• To ensure easy cutting, always let baked lasagna rest for at least 5 minutes after being removed from the oven.
• Cut lasagna with a very sharp serrated knife.
• Leftovers? Once baked and refrigerated, lasagna reheats beautifully...and the flavor even improves! If you are reheating in the oven, be sure to spread extra sauce on top of the lasagna if it looks dry. The microwave is an even better way of reheating lasagna. Lasagna can be tightly wrapped and frozen. Defrost in the refrigerator before reheating.

LASAGNA
RECIPES
L

CLASSIC LASAGNA

- 6 long lasagna noodles, uncooked
- 1 pkg. The Turkey Store® Hot or Sweet Lean Italian Sausage
- 1 jar (28 oz.) spaghetti sauce or 3½ cups homemade spaghetti sauce (see page 13)
- 1 container (15 oz.) ricotta cheese
- ¼ cup chopped fresh basil or Italian parsley
- ½ cup grated Parmesan or Romano cheese
- 2 cups (8 oz.) shredded mozzarella or Italian blend cheese

Heat oven to 350 degrees. Cook noodles according to package directions. Meanwhile, crumble sausage into a large skillet, discarding casings. Cook over medium heat 5 minutes, stirring occasionally. Add spaghetti sauce; simmer uncovered 10 minutes. Combine ricotta cheese, basil and 1/4 cup Parmesan cheese; mix well.

Spoon 3/4 cup spaghetti sauce mixture over bottom of a 13 x 9-inch baking dish. Layer half of cooked noodles over sauce; top with half of ricotta cheese mixture. Sprinkle with 1 cup mozzarella cheese; top with 1 cup spaghetti sauce. Repeat layering with remaining ricotta cheese mixture, 3 noodles and remaining spaghetti sauce. Top with remaining 1 cup mozzarella cheese and remaining 1/4 cup Parmesan cheese. Cover with foil; bake 50 minutes. Uncover; continue baking 10 minutes or until bubbly. Let stand 5 minutes before serving.
Makes 8 servings.

Nutrition information per serving: Calories: 360, Protein: 28g, Carbohydrates: 24g, Fat: 17g, Cholesterol: 66mg, Sodium: 1,046mg

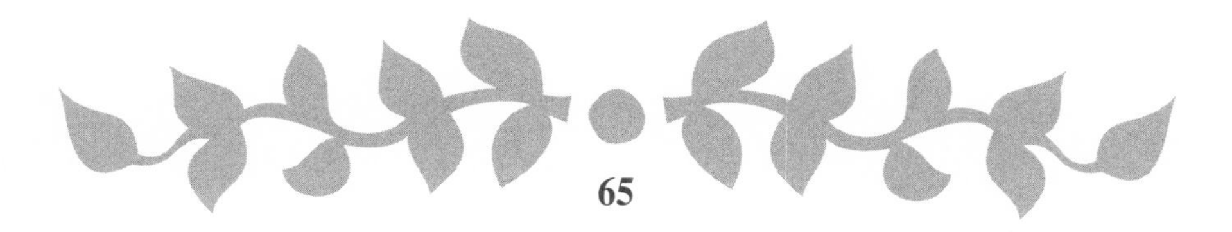

LASAGNA FLORENTINE

- 6 long lasagna noodles, uncooked
- 1 pkg. The Turkey Store® Extra Lean Ground Breast
- 2 teaspoons bottled or fresh minced garlic
- 1 jar (28 oz.) spaghetti sauce
- 1 container (15 oz.) ricotta cheese
- 1 large egg
- 1 pkg. (10 oz.) frozen chopped spinach, thawed, well drained
- ¼ to ½ teaspoon crushed red pepper flakes, as desired
- ⅛ teaspoon nutmeg
- 2 cups (8 oz.) shredded mozzarella or Italian blend cheese

Heat oven to 350 degrees. Cook noodles according to package directions. Meanwhile, cook turkey and garlic in a large skillet over medium heat until turkey is no longer pink, stirring occasionally. Add spaghetti sauce; simmer 10 minutes, stirring occasionally. Combine ricotta cheese, egg, spinach, pepper flakes and nutmeg; mix well.

Spread 1/2 cup spaghetti sauce mixture in bottom of a 13 x 9-inch baking dish. Layer half of noodles over sauce; spoon cheese mixture over noodles. Spoon 1 cup sauce over cheese; repeat layering with remaining noodles, cheese mixture and sauce. Cover with foil; bake 50 minutes or until bubbly. Sprinkle mozzarella cheese over lasagna; return to oven and continue baking 5 minutes or until cheese is melted.

Makes 8 servings.

Nutrition information per serving: Calories: 346, Protein: 36g, Carbohydrates: 26g, Fat: 12g, Cholesterol: 94mg, Sodium: 571mg

QUICK & EASY LASAGNA

- 1 pkg. The Turkey Store® Hot or Sweet Lean Italian Sausage
- 1 jar (26 oz.) tomato and basil or mushroom spaghetti sauce
- 6 (7 x 4 inch) no-boil lasagna noodles
- 1 container (15 oz.) ricotta cheese
- ¼ cup grated Parmesan cheese
- 2 cups (8 oz.) shredded mozzarella cheese

Heat oven to 450 degrees. Crumble sausage into a large saucepan; discard casings. Cook over medium-high heat 5 minutes, breaking sausage into chunks and stirring frequently. Add spaghetti sauce; bring to a boil. Reduce heat; simmer uncovered 5 minutes, stirring occasionally.

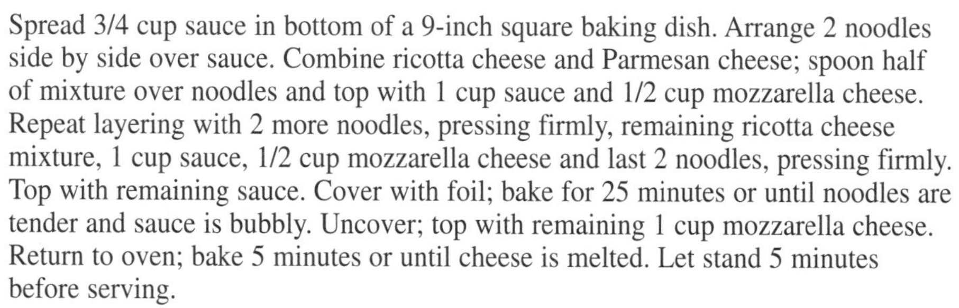

Spread 3/4 cup sauce in bottom of a 9-inch square baking dish. Arrange 2 noodles side by side over sauce. Combine ricotta cheese and Parmesan cheese; spoon half of mixture over noodles and top with 1 cup sauce and 1/2 cup mozzarella cheese. Repeat layering with 2 more noodles, pressing firmly, remaining ricotta cheese mixture, 1 cup sauce, 1/2 cup mozzarella cheese and last 2 noodles, pressing firmly. Top with remaining sauce. Cover with foil; bake for 25 minutes or until noodles are tender and sauce is bubbly. Uncover; top with remaining 1 cup mozzarella cheese. Return to oven; bake 5 minutes or until cheese is melted. Let stand 5 minutes before serving.

Makes 6 servings.

Nutrition information per serving: Calories: 409, Protein: 33g, Carbohydrates: 16g, Fat: 24g, Cholesterol: 89mg, Sodium: 1,376mg

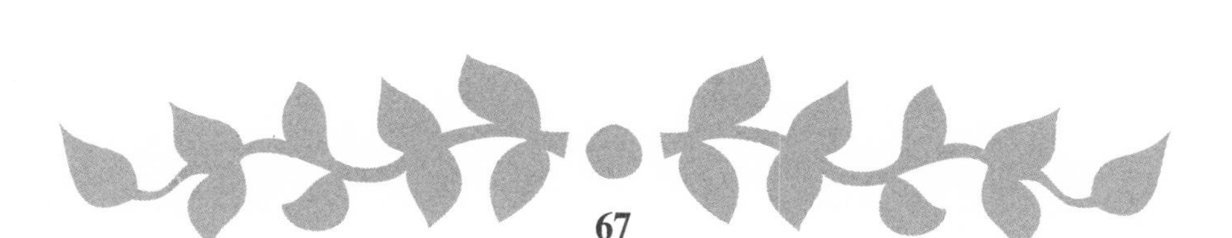

Light Lasagna Florentine

- 6 long lasagna noodles, uncooked
- 1 pkg. The Turkey Store® Extra Lean Ground Breast
- 2 teaspoons bottled or fresh minced garlic
- 1 jar (28 oz.) light spaghetti sauce
- 1 container (15 oz.) fat free ricotta cheese
- 1 egg white
- 1 pkg. (10 oz.) frozen chopped spinach, thawed and well drained
- ¼ to ½ teaspoon crushed red pepper flakes, as desired
- ⅛ teaspoon nutmeg
- 1 cup (4 oz.) reduced fat shredded mozzarella cheese

Heat oven to 350 degrees. Cook noodles according to package directions, omitting salt. Meanwhile, cook turkey and garlic in a large skillet over medium heat until turkey is no longer pink, stirring occasionally. Add spaghetti sauce; simmer 10 minutes, stirring occasionally. Combine ricotta cheese, egg white, spinach, pepper flakes and nutmeg; mix well.

Spread 1/2 cup spaghetti sauce mixture in bottom of a 13 x 9-inch baking dish. Layer half of noodles over sauce; spoon ricotta cheese mixture over noodles. Spoon 1 cup sauce over cheese; repeat layering with remaining noodles, cheese mixture and sauce. Cover with foil; bake 50 minutes or until bubbly. Sprinkle mozzarella cheese over lasagna; return to oven and continue baking 5 minutes or until cheese is melted.

Makes 8 servings.

Nutrition information per serving: Calories: 268, Protein: 30g, Carbohydrates: 28g, Fat: 3g, Cholesterol: 48mg, Sodium: 431mg

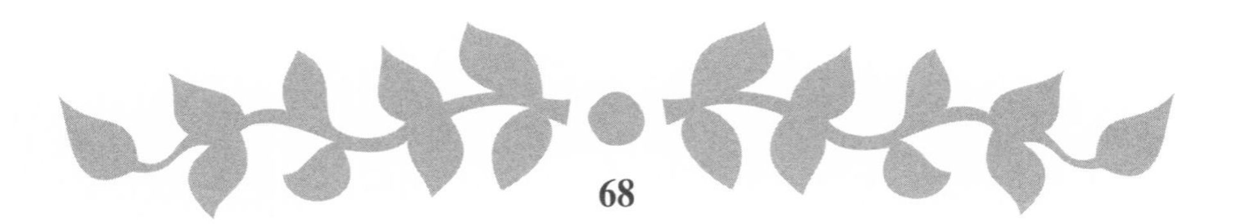

FOOD FOR THOUGHT

BREAKFAST AND BRUNCH RECIPES

Did You Know That?

The word breakfast means, literally, to break fast, a fitting way to describe the first meal of the day after a night filled with sleep but not food. Americans have made many breakfast foods famous: cold cereals are one, pancakes another. By 1796 pancakes appear in the first published American cookbook by Amelia Simmons. Brunch, a meal that combines breakfast and lunch, was a British invention, first introduced in 1895. By the next year, 1896, The London magazine Punch informed readers that "To be fashionable nowadays we must 'brunch.'"

Menu Makers

- Garnish Breakfast Muffin Sandwiches with skewers of strawberries, cubed melon, seedless grapes, nectarine slices or other seasonal fruit.
- Sausage & Sassy Scrambled Eggs pair perfectly with hot biscuits and a frosty pitcher of orange juice. A nice touch: serve three varieties of jam or jelly.
- Pigs in a Blanket are good for brunch as well as breakfast. Serve them with poached or fried eggs and wedges of a sweet, seedless navel orange.
- Huevos Rancheros, a hearty breakfast or brunch dish, may be served with a side of low-fat canned refried beans simply reheated in the microwave or in a skillet. Garnish plate with a skewer of banana chunks sprinkled with cinnamon sugar, or sliced, ripe avocado. And offer a bottle of hot red pepper sauce.
- Serve Fire & Ice Brunch Bake with cornbread and a big scoop of applesauce or cranberry-apple sauce.

Tips and Tricks

- Egg safety depends upon how eggs are handled and cooked. Be careful that the raw egg inside the shell does not come in contact with the outer shell when cracking eggs. Wash hands, any kitchen utensils and counter surfaces that come in contact with raw eggs. Always cook eggs to a temperature of 140°F. Measure with an instant-read thermometer or use the following criteria: egg whites become firm and white at 160°F and the yolk begins to thicken and set at 145°F (the yolk center may still be runny at 145°F). Scrambled eggs, omelets or other preparations made with beaten whole eggs, start to firm and set at 165°F.
- Egg quality depends not only on freshness but on how they are stored. A date or freshness code appears on all cartons of USDA-inspected eggs. Always purchase eggs from a refrigerated case and refrigerate them immediately at home.
- Signs of freshness include round, high yolks and thick, cloudy, cohesive whites. The older the egg, the flatter the yolk becomes and the thinner and clearer the whites. To check freshness, place uncooked eggs in their shells in a pan or bowl with several inches of cold water. If an egg floats, discard it. The interior moisture has evaporated and the egg has shrunk.

BREAKFAST
RECIPES
B

Breakfast Muffin Sandwiches

1 pkg. The Turkey Store® Mild Breakfast Sausage Patties
1 tablespoon butter or margarine
6 large eggs
½ teaspoon salt
¼ teaspoon freshly ground black pepper
½ cup (2 oz.) shredded cheddar cheese
6 English muffins, split, lightly toasted

Cook sausage according to package directions. Meanwhile, melt butter in a large nonstick skillet over medium heat. Crack eggs into skillet. Sprinkle eggs with salt and pepper; cook 2 minutes. Cover skillet; cook 3 to 4 minutes or until whites of eggs are set. Sprinkle with cheese; cover and cook 1 minute or until cheese is melted. Place 2 sausage patties on each muffin bottom; top with one egg and close sandwiches with muffin tops.

Makes 6 servings.

Nutrition information per serving: Calories: 414, Protein: 23g, Carbohydrates: 28g, Fat: 23g, Cholesterol: 278mg, Sodium: 993mg

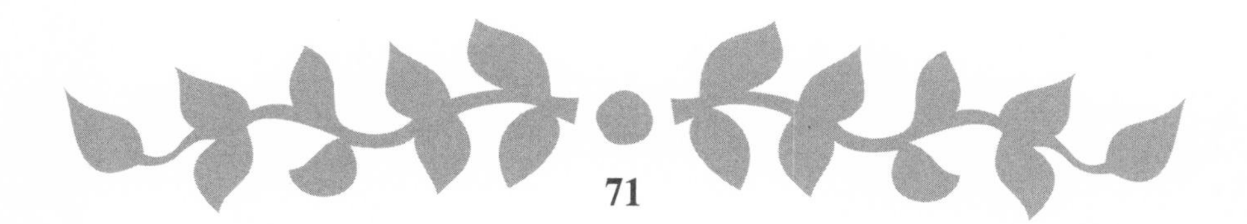

SAUSAGE & SASSY SCRAMBLED EGGS

- 1 pkg. The Turkey Store® Breakfast Sausage Links
- 2 tablespoons butter or margarine
- 10 large eggs
- ¼ cup 2% lowfat milk
- ½ cup finely diced red bell pepper
- ½ cup thinly sliced green onions
- ¾ teaspoon salt
- ¾ teaspoon hot pepper sauce
- ½ cup (2 oz.) shredded cheddar cheese

Cook sausages according to package directions. Meanwhile, melt butter in a large deep skillet over medium-high heat. In a medium bowl, beat together eggs, milk, bell pepper, green onions, salt and pepper sauce. Pour into skillet. Cook, stirring occasionally, until eggs are set, 5 to 6 minutes; sprinkle with cheese and serve with sausages.

Makes 7 servings.

Nutrition information per serving: Calories: 317, Protein: 20g, Carbohydrates: 3g, Fat: 23g, Cholesterol: 367mg, Sodium: 768mg

PIGS IN A BLANKET

- 1 pkg. The Turkey Store® Breakfast Sausage Links
- 1-½ cups all-purpose flour
- 3 tablespoons sugar
- 1-½ teaspoons baking powder
- ½ teaspoon salt
- ½ teaspoon baking soda
- 2 cups buttermilk
- 3 tablespoons butter or margarine, melted
- 2 large eggs, beaten
- Cooking spray
- 1 tablespoon powdered sugar
- 1 cup pure maple syrup

Heat oven to 350 degrees. Cook sausage according to package directions. Meanwhile, in a large bowl, combine flour, sugar, baking powder, salt and baking soda; mix well. Add buttermilk, melted butter and eggs; mix just until dry ingredients are moistened. Heat a nonstick griddle or large skillet over medium heat until hot. (If griddle is not nonstick, coat with cooking spray or a thin film of vegetable oil.) Drop batter by 1/4 cupfuls onto hot griddle. Cook until some of the bubbles that appear on the pancake surface have popped and bottom is golden brown. Turn; continue cooking until bottom is golden brown. Transfer pancakes as they are cooked to a wire cooling rack.

Coat a 13 x 9-inch baking dish with cooking spray. Roll up cooked sausage link in each pancake; place seam side down in prepared dish. Cover with foil; bake about 15 minutes or until heated through. Place powdered sugar in a sifter or strainer; shake evenly over pancake rolls. Serve immediately with syrup.
Makes 7 servings.

Nutrition information per serving: Calories: 475, Protein: 15g, Carbohydrates: 62g, Fat: 18g, Cholesterol: 122mg, Sodium: 853mg

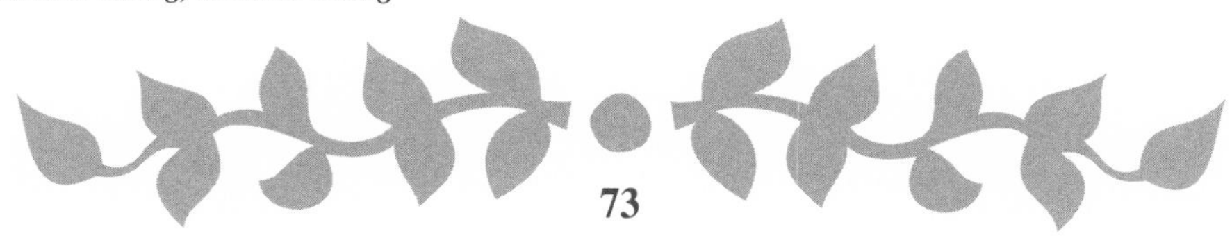

HUEVOS RANCHEROS

- 1 pkg. The Turkey Store® Mild Breakfast Sausage Patties
- ¼ cup vegetable oil
- 6 corn tortillas
- 2 tablespoons butter or margarine
- 6 large eggs
- Salt (optional)
- ¾ cup salsa or picante sauce
- ¼ cup catsup
- 1 cup (4 oz.) Shredded Mexican blend cheese or Monterey jack cheese
- ¼ cup chopped cilantro (optional)

Cook sausage according to package directions. Meanwhile, heat oil in a large skillet over medium-high heat until very hot. Fry tortillas one at a time in hot oil until lightly brown and crisp, about 1 minute per side. Transfer to paper towels to drain. Arrange tortillas on serving plates; top each tortilla with 2 cooked sausage patties.

Melt 1 tablespoon butter in same skillet. Fry 3 eggs sunny-side-up or over-easy as desired. Sprinkle with salt, if desired. Place one egg over each serving of sausages. Repeat with remaining 1 tablespoon butter and 3 eggs. Add salsa and catsup to skillet; heat through, stirring constantly. Spoon mixture over each serving; top with cheese and, if desired, cilantro.

Makes 6 servings.

Nutrition information per serving: Calories: 502, Protein: 23g, Carbohydrates: 20g, Fat: 37g, Cholesterol: 293mg, Sodium: 958mg

Fire & Ice Brunch Bake

- 1 cup uncooked white rice, preferably converted
- 1 pkg. The Turkey Store® Smoke Seasoned Lean Sausage or Lean Bratwurst
- ¾ cup thick and chunky salsa
- ½ cup light or regular sour cream
- 1-½ cups (6 oz.) shredded cheddar cheese
- 6 large eggs
- Salt and pepper (optional)

Cook rice according to package directions. Meanwhile, heat oven to 350 degrees. Crumble sausage into a large skillet; discard casings. Cook over medium heat, breaking sausage into chunks, about 8 minutes or until sausage is no longer pink. Stir sausage into cooked rice. Add salsa and sour cream; mix well. Stir in 1 cup cheese. Spread mixture evenly in a greased 13 x 9-inch baking dish.

Using a 1/4 cup metal measuring cup, make 6 deep indentations in rice mixture. Break one egg into each indentation; sprinkle with salt and pepper, if desired. Bake 15 minutes; sprinkle with remaining 1/2 cup cheese. Continue baking 8 to 10 minutes or until mixture is hot and eggs are just set in center. Serve with additional salsa, if desired.

Makes 6 servings.

Nutrition information per serving: Calories: 458, Protein: 28g, Carbohydrates: 28g, Fat: 24g, Cholesterol: 307mg, Sodium: 939mg

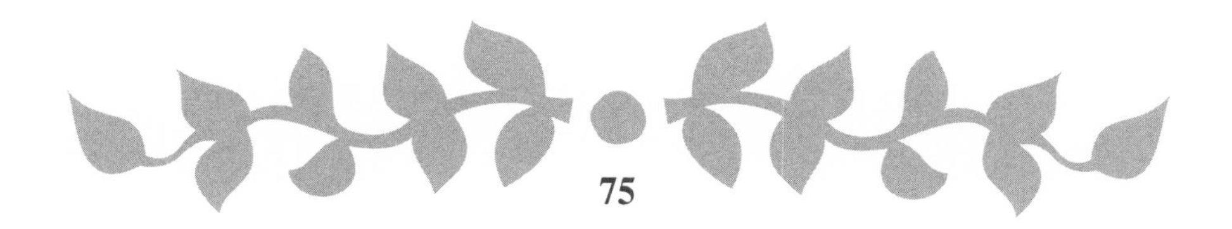

LIGHT SAUSAGE & SASSY SCRAMBLED EGGS

- 1 pkg. The Turkey Store® Breakfast Sausage Links
- Butter-flavor cooking spray
- 2-½ cups liquid egg substitute or 8 large egg whites plus 2 large eggs
- ¼ cup skim milk
- ½ cup finely diced red bell pepper
- ½ cup thinly sliced green onions
- ¾ teaspoon salt (optional)
- ¾ teaspoon hot pepper sauce
- ½ cup (2 oz.) shredded low-fat cheddar cheese

Cook sausages according to package directions. Meanwhile, coat a large deep nonstick skillet with cooking spray; heat over medium-high heat. In a medium bowl, beat together egg substitute, milk, bell pepper, green onions, salt, if desired, and pepper sauce. Pour into skillet. Cook, stirring occasionally, until eggs are set, 5 to 6 minutes; sprinkle with cheese and serve with sausages.

Makes 7 servings.

Nutrition information per serving: Calories: 210, Protein: 19g, Carbohydrates: 4g, Fat: 12g, Cholesterol: 48mg, Sodium: 580mg

FOOD FOR THOUGHT

PIZZA RECIPES

Did You Know That?

The word pizza means "pie," and pizza is as dear to our hearts as apple pie. Pizza was created in the 17th century in Naples, Italy, where the first pizzeria opened in 1830. The first pizzas were simply yeast dough topped with tomatoes. By the 19th century, mozzarella cheese was added. The most famous Italian pizza, Pizza Margherita, was made from tomatoes, mozzarella and fresh basil to represent the colors of the Italian flag in honor of the 1889 visit of Queen Margherita to Naples. Pizza was brought to America by immigrants from Naples, and the first American pizza parlor of record was Gennaro Lombardi's, which opened in New York in 1905. Since then, pizza has taken on hundreds of different toppings and several different shapes and sizes. Chicago-style deep-dish pizza was created in 1943 by Ike Sewell and Ric Riccardo at Pizzeria Uno. So-called designer pizzas with toppings such as smoked salmon were first created in 1982 by Chef Wolfgang Puck at his Los Angeles restaurant Spago. The world's largest pizza—so far—was 10,000 square feet and baked in 1991 by Lorenzo Amato, proprietor, Cafe di Lorenzo, Tallahassee, Florida.

Menu Makers

- Serve Sausage Pizza with little dishes of red pepper flakes, dried oregano and grated Parmesan cheese for extra topping at the table.
- All any pizza needs to make a meal is a large salad. But the salad can take its cue from the pizza:
  - Pair Sausage Pizza with a traditional green salad with Italian herb or balsamic vinaigrette.
  - Mediterranean-Style Pizza calls for a salad of romaine lettuce with a lemon juice-garlic-olive oil dressing.
  - Thai Style Pizza is complemented by a salad of mixed greens combined with drained, chopped water chestnuts, bamboo shoots and Mandarin orange segments. Toss with honey-mustard vinaigrette.

Tips and Tricks

- Pizza may be cut with a traditional pizza wheel, but sharp kitchen scissors work just as well.
- Sliding cooked pizza off pan and onto a large cutting board makes cutting easier. Cut pizza wedges may be returned to pan with spatula for serving.
- A large wooden or aluminum pizza peel with a long handle is a useful piece of kitchen equipment that makes easy work of sliding pizza in and out of the hot oven.
- Round cardboard pizza disks, available at restaurant supply houses, are not only nice for serving pizzas, but help prevent crust from becoming soggy as steam from cooking is released.

PIZZA
RECIPES

SAUSAGE PIZZA

- 1 pkg. The Turkey Store® Sweet Lean Italian Sausage
- 1 medium green or yellow bell pepper, chopped
- 3 small (7 inch) or 1 large (12 inch) prepared pizza crust
- ½ cup prepared pizza sauce
- 2 cups (8 oz.) shredded mozzarella or Italian blend cheese
- 2 thin slices red onion, separated into rings (optional)
- Chopped fresh basil (optional)

Heat oven to 450 degrees. Remove and discard casing from sausage. Cook sausage and bell pepper in a large nonstick skillet over medium-high heat 8 minutes or until sausage is no longer pink in center, breaking sausage into chunks with a wooden spoon and stirring occasionally. Drain well.

Place pizza crusts on a large cookie sheet. Spread sauce over crusts; top with half of cheese. Top with sausage mixture and, if desired, onion rings; sprinkle with remaining cheese. Bake 10 to 12 minutes or until crust is golden brown and cheese is melted. Sprinkle with basil, if desired.
Makes 6 servings.

Nutrition information per serving: Calories: 429, Protein: 29g, Carbohydrates: 39g, Fat: 17g, Cholesterol: 59mg, Sodium: 1,135mg

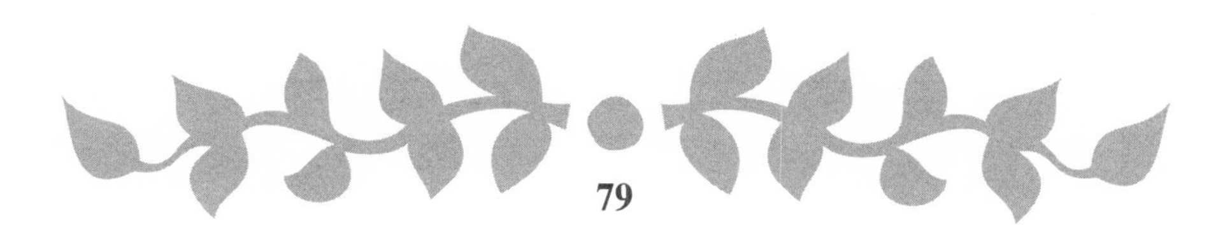

THAI PIZZA

- 1 pkg. The Turkey Store® Breast Strips
- 2 teaspoons bottled or fresh minced ginger
- 2 teaspoons bottled or fresh minced garlic
- ¼ teaspoon crushed red pepper flakes
- Cooking spray
- ¼ cup hoisin or stir-fry sauce
- ⅓ cup thinly sliced green onions
- ½ teaspoon finely grated lime peel
- 1 large (12 inch) prepared pizza crust
- ⅓ cup coarsely chopped roasted peanuts
- 2 tablespoons chopped cilantro or basil

Heat oven to 450 degrees. Toss turkey strips with ginger, garlic and pepper flakes. Coat a large nonstick skillet with cooking spray; heat over medium-high heat. Add turkey; stir-fry 2 minutes. Add hoisin sauce; stir-fry 2 minutes. Place pizza crust on a large cookie sheet. Spread mixture evenly over pizza crust; sprinkle with green onions and lime peel. Bake 8 to 10 minutes or until crust is golden brown and hot. Sprinkle with peanuts and cilantro. Cut into wedges.

Makes 6 main dish or 12 appetizer servings.

Nutrition information per serving: Calories: 347, Protein: 29g, Carbohydrates: 40g, Fat: 9g, Cholesterol: 36mg, Sodium: 694mg

MEDITERRANEAN PIZZA

1 tablespoon olive oil
4 cloves garlic, thinly sliced
1 pkg. The Turkey Store® Breast Strips
½ teaspoon dried rosemary, crushed
¼ teaspoon salt
¼ teaspoon crushed red pepper flakes
1 (12 inch) prepared pizza crust
2 large ripe tomatoes or 4 plum tomatoes, thinly sliced
½ cup pitted and halved Kalamata or ripe olives
1 cup (4 oz.) crumbled goat or feta cheese
¼ cup thinly sliced basil leaves

PIZZA RECIPES

Heat oven to 450 degrees. Heat oil in a large skillet over medium-high heat; add garlic and cook 2 minutes or until edges are golden brown. Add turkey strips; sprinkle with rosemary, salt and pepper flakes. Stir-fry 2 minutes or just until no longer pink. (Do not overcook; turkey will continue to cook in oven.) Drain well.

Place pizza crust on a large cookie sheet; top with tomatoes, the turkey mixture, olives and goat cheese. Bake about 10 minutes or until crust is golden brown and turkey is no longer pink in center. Sprinkle with basil; cut into wedges.
Makes 6 main dish servings or 12 appetizer servings.

Nutrition information per main dish serving: Calories: 442, Protein: 35g, Carbohydrates: 37g, Fat: 18g, Cholesterol: 59mg, Sodium: 785mg

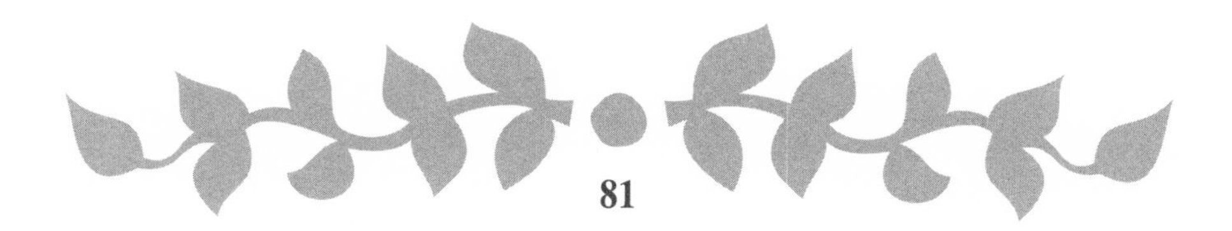

LIGHT MEDITERRANEAN PIZZA

Cooking spray
4 cloves garlic, minced
1 pkg. The Turkey Store® Breast Strips
½ teaspoon dried rosemary, crushed
¼ teaspoon salt
¼ teaspoon crushed red pepper flakes
1 (12 inch) prepared thin pizza crust
2 large ripe tomatoes or 4 plum tomatoes, thinly sliced
¼ cup pitted and halved Kalamata or ripe olives
¾ cup (3 oz.) crumbled feta cheese
¼ cup thinly sliced basil leaves

Heat oven to 450 degrees. Coat a large skillet with cooking spray. Heat over medium-high heat; add garlic and cook 1 minute. Add turkey strips; sprinkle with rosemary, salt and pepper flakes. Stir-fry 2 minutes or just until no longer pink. (Do not overcook; turkey will continue to cook in oven.)

Place pizza crust on a large cookie sheet; top with tomatoes, the turkey mixture, olives and feta cheese. Bake about 10 minutes or until crust is golden brown and turkey is no longer pink in center. Sprinkle with basil; cut into wedges.

Makes 6 main dish or 12 appetizer servings.

Nutrition information per serving: Calories: 293, Protein: 31g, Carbohydrates: 24g, Fat: 8g, Cholesterol: 61mg, Sodium: 619mg

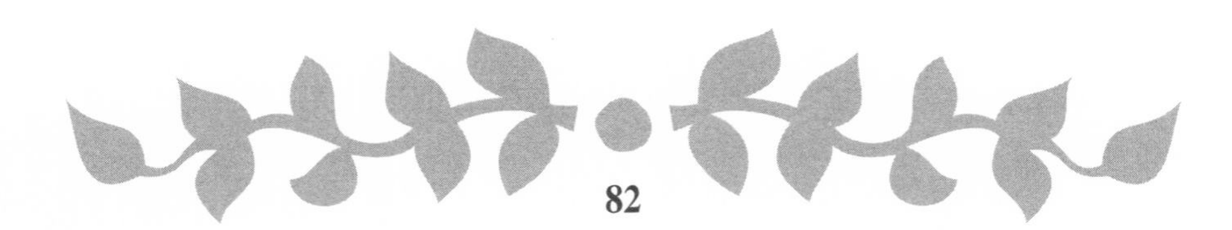

SALAD RECIPES

Did You Know That?

The word salad comes from the Latin word sal (salt) because early salads were seasoned mainly with salt. Traditionally, salad was a side dish. Americans serve theirs before the main course; the French serve theirs after the main and before the cheese course. Famous American salad creations include the Waldorf, Cobb and Caesar salads. But with the advent of the chef's salad, salads moved to center stage. Today, main-dish or entree salads are a standard feature on most restaurant menus and in many home-cooked meals.

Menu Makers

- Soup and bread are the only side dishes needed for terrific main-dish salad menus.
- With Chef's Salad Supreme, serve minestrone or garden vegetable soup with a crusty loaf of Italian bread.
- With Grilled Caesar Salad, start with tomato or garden vegetable soup and add San Francisco sourdough bread.
- Asian Noodle Salad calls for Japanese miso soup (available in ready-to-make packages at the supermarket) and egg rolls (available frozen). Or else, stop by your local Thai or Chinese restaurant and pick up Tom Yum (Thai hot and sour shrimp soup) and spring rolls or egg drop soup and pot stickers.
- With Southwestern Rice Salad, serve either corn chowder or gazpacho along with warmed corn or flour tortillas or hot corn bread.
- Wonderful Waldorf Salad goes well with hot potato soup or cold vichyssoise and whole grain rolls or hearth-baked walnut-raisin bread.

Tips and Tricks

- For food safety's sake, it's a good idea to rinse all lettuce well, including ready-to-use packaged salad greens. Rinse well in cold, running water and spin in a salad spinner to remove excess water.
- Ready-to-use packaged greens are a great convenience. But if you have time, consider mixing two or three of the following: romaine (it has six times as much Vitamin C and eight times as much Vitamin A as iceberg lettuce); spinach and baby spinach; Bibb and Boston; arugula (nicely bitter used in small quantities); and radicchio (Italian chicory that, in small quantities, lends flavor and color to salads).
- Always add dressing to salads right before serving. Moisten, don't drown, a salad in dressing. Toss well to distribute, so ingredients are lightly coated.
- To crisp salad greens, place rinsed, spin-dried greens in salad bowl, cover with plastic wrap and refrigerate for one hour before adding other ingredients and dressing.

SALAD
RECIPES

Asian Noodle Salad

- 1 pkg. The Turkey Store® Boneless Breast Tenderloins
- ¼ cup plus 3 tablespoons soy sauce
- 2 teaspoons bottled or fresh minced garlic
- 2 tablespoons peanut butter
- 3 tablespoons vegetable oil
- 2 tablespoons seasoned rice vinegar
- 2 teaspoons dark sesame oil
- 1-½ teaspoons bottled or fresh minced ginger
- ¾ teaspoon hot chili oil or 1/2 teaspoon crushed red pepper flakes
- 8 ounces vermicelli or thin spaghetti, broken in half
- ½ cup packaged julienne-cut carrots
- 1 red bell pepper, cut into short, thin strips
- 1-½ cups fresh snow pea pods, cut lengthwise into thin strips
- ½ cup diagonally sliced green onions (optional)

Place tenderloins in a plastic bag. Add 3 tablespoons soy sauce and garlic; close bag securely, turning to coat. Refrigerate at least 30 minutes or up to 4 hours. Prepare barbecue grill.

In a large bowl, whisk together peanut butter and vegetable oil. Whisk in remaining 1/4 cup soy sauce, vinegar, sesame oil, ginger and chili oil. Cook vermicelli according to package directions. Combine carrots and bell pepper in microwave safe dish. Cover and cook at high power 1 minute. Add snow peas; cover and continue cooking 1 minute or until crisp-tender. (Or, vegetables may be blanched in boiling water just until crisp-tender.) Drain vermicelli; add to soy sauce mixture in bowl. Add vegetables; toss well. Drain tenderloins, reserving marinade. Grill over medium coals 12 to 14 minutes or until no longer pink in center, turning occasionally and brushing with reserved marinade during the first 6 minutes of cooking. Transfer to carving board; cut each tenderloin lengthwise in half and then cut crosswise into 1/4-inch-thick slices. Add turkey and, if desired, green onions to noodle mixture; toss well. *Makes 6 servings.*

Nutrition information per serving: Calories: 405, Protein: 31g, Carbohydrates: 40g, Fat: 14g, Cholesterol: 44mg, Sodium: 1,214mg

CHEF'S SALAD SUPREME

- 1 pkg. The Turkey Store® Breast Strips
- 2 teaspoons Creole, Cajun or Mexican seasonings
- 1 tablespoon garlic-infused or extra virgin olive oil
- 8 cups packed assorted torn salad greens
- 3 slices (3 oz.) cheddar or muenster cheese, cut into short, thin strips
- 2 hard-cooked eggs, peeled, sliced
- 1 cup halved cherry tomatoes or diced tomato
- ½ cup yellow or red bell pepper strips
- ½ cup herb or garlic croutons
- ⅔ cup prepared Thousand Island dressing
- Freshly ground black pepper to taste

Toss turkey strips with seasonings. Heat oil in a large skillet over medium-high heat. Add turkey strips; stir-fry 3 minutes or until no longer pink in center. Transfer to a bowl; set aside to cool or refrigerate until serving time. In a large bowl, combine greens, cheese, eggs, tomatoes, bell pepper strips and croutons. Add cooled turkey and dressing; toss well. Arrange on 4 chilled serving plates; top with pepper.
Makes 4 servings.

Nutrition information per serving: Calories: 529, Protein: 42g, Carbohydrates: 18g, Fat: 32g, Cholesterol: 210mg, Sodium: 941mg

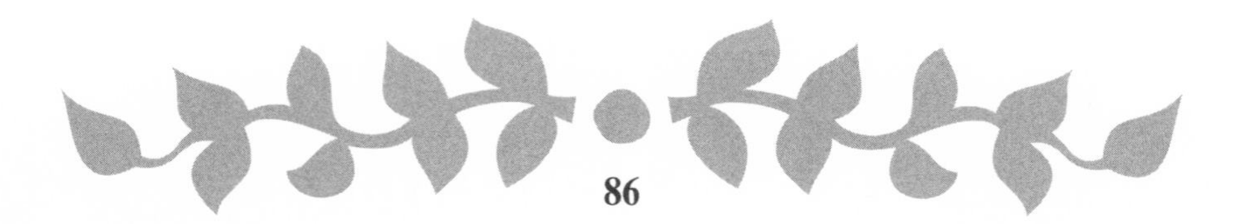

Grilled Caesar Salad

1 pkg. The Turkey Store® Breast Cutlets
⅓ cup plus 3 tablespoons bottled Caesar salad dressing (oil & vinegar base, not creamy)
8 cups packed sliced romaine lettuce
1 cup garlic or garlic and herb croutons
¼ cup grated Parmesan cheese
½ teaspoon freshly ground black pepper

Place cutlets in a shallow dish or plastic bag. Pour 3 tablespoons dressing over cutlets, turning to coat. Cover dish or close bag securely; marinate in refrigerator at least 30 minutes or up to 4 hours. Prepare barbecue grill.

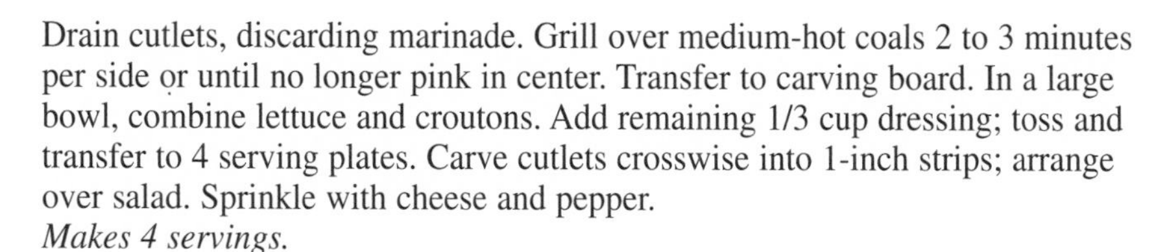

Drain cutlets, discarding marinade. Grill over medium-hot coals 2 to 3 minutes per side or until no longer pink in center. Transfer to carving board. In a large bowl, combine lettuce and croutons. Add remaining 1/3 cup dressing; toss and transfer to 4 serving plates. Carve cutlets crosswise into 1-inch strips; arrange over salad. Sprinkle with cheese and pepper.

Makes 4 servings.

Nutrition information per serving: Calories: 309, Protein: 36g, Carbohydrates: 10g, Fat: 15g, Cholesterol: 80mg, Sodium: 691mg

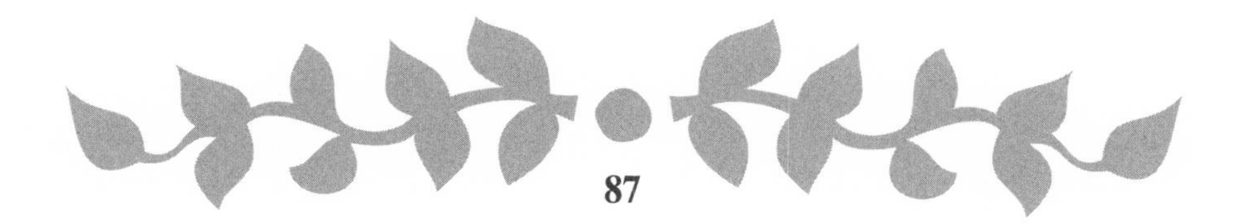

SOUTHWESTERN RICE SALAD

- 1 pkg. The Turkey Store® Breast Cutlets
- 2 teaspoons Mexican seasoning or chili powder
- 1 cup hot or medium salsa
- 2-½ cups chilled, cooked converted white rice
- 1 cup rinsed and drained canned black beans
- 1 red or yellow bell pepper, diced
- 1 cup (4 oz.) diced or shredded sharp cheddar cheese
- ½ cup thinly sliced green onions
- ⅓ cup chopped cilantro
- 2 tablespoons vegetable oil
- ½ teaspoon bottled minced garlic

Sprinkle both sides of cutlets with Mexican seasoning. Place in a plastic bag; add 1/2 cup salsa. Close bag, turning to coat. Refrigerate at least 30 minutes or up to 2 hours.

In a large bowl, combine rice, beans, bell pepper, cheese, green onions and cilantro. Combine remaining 1/2 cup salsa, oil and garlic; mix well. Add to rice mixture; toss well. Cover; refrigerate until serving time. Prepare barbecue grill or heat a ridged non-stick skillet over medium heat. Drain cutlets, discarding marinade. Grill over medium coals or pan-broil in skillet about 3 minutes per side or until no longer pink in center. Transfer to carving board; cool at least 5 minutes. Cut into 1/2-inch cubes; add to salad, tossing well. *Makes 6 servings.*

Nutrition information per serving: Calories: 384, Protein: 31g, Carbohydrates: 33g, Fat: 13g, Cholesterol: 63mg, Sodium: 600mg

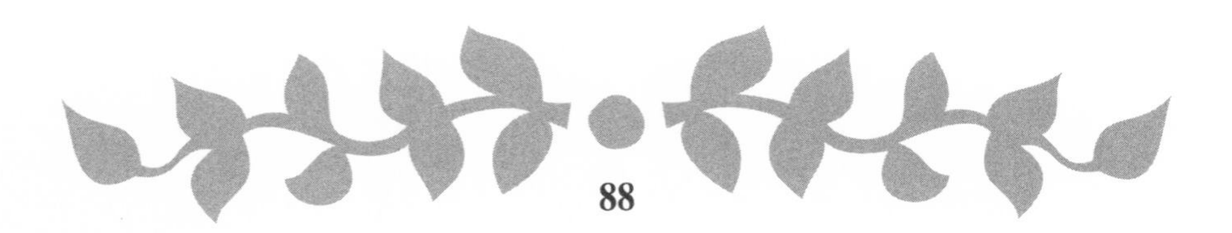

WONDERFUL WALDORF SALAD

- 1 can (13-¾ oz.) chicken broth
- 1 pkg. The Turkey Store® Boneless Breast Tenderloins
- ½ cup light or regular mayonnaise
- 1 tablespoon fresh lemon juice
- ¼ teaspoon salt
- ¼ teaspoon freshly ground black pepper
- 1 cup diced unpeeled red apple
- ½ cup thinly sliced celery
- ⅓ cup coarsely chopped walnuts, toasted
- Red leaf or Boston lettuce leaves

Bring broth to a simmer in a large deep skillet. Add turkey; cover and simmer 8 minutes. Turn turkey; cover and continue to simmer about 10 minutes or until no longer pink in center. Remove from heat; let stand uncovered 10 minutes. Transfer to a carving board; cut into 1/2-inch cubes. (Refrigerate or freeze broth for another use.) In a large bowl, combine mayonnaise, lemon juice, salt and pepper. Add turkey, apple, celery and walnuts; toss well. Serve immediately or cover and chill. Serve on lettuce leaves with additional freshly ground pepper, if desired.

Makes 6 servings.

Nutrition information per serving: Calories: 255, Protein: 26g, Carbohydrates: 7g, Fat: 14g, Cholesterol: 57mg, Sodium: 608mg

LIGHT CHEF'S SALAD

SALAD RECIPES

- 1 pkg. The Turkey Store® Breast Strips
- 2 teaspoons Creole, Cajun or Mexican seasonings
- 1 teaspoon bottled or fresh minced garlic
- Cooking spray
- 8 cups packed assorted torn salad greens
- ½ cup lowfat shredded cheddar cheese
- 2 hard-cooked egg whites, coarsely chopped
- 1 cup halved cherry tomatoes or diced tomato
- ½ cup yellow or red bell pepper strips
- ¼ cup herb or garlic croutons
- ⅔ cup fat-free Thousand Island dressing
- Freshly ground black pepper to taste

Toss turkey strips with seasonings and garlic. Coat a large non-stick skillet with cooking spray. Heat at medium-high. Add turkey strips; stir-fry 3 minutes or until no longer pink in center. Transfer to a bowl; set aside to cool or refrigerate until serving time. In a large bowl, combine greens, cheese, egg whites, tomatoes, bell pepper strips and croutons. Add cooled turkey and dressing; toss well. Arrange on 4 chilled serving plates; top with pepper.

Makes 4 servings.

Nutrition information per serving: Calories: 277, Protein: 38g, Carbohydrates: 21g, Fat: 5g, Cholesterol: 65mg, Sodium: 954mg

FOOD FOR THOUGHT

SCALOPPINI RECIPES

Did You Know That?

Scaloppini, in Italian cuisine, refers to thin slices or scallops of meat that are either dredged in flour or dipped in beaten egg, breaded, sautéed and served with a sauce. Schnitzel, in German cuisine, also refers to thin cutlets, dipped in beaten egg, then dredged in flour and/or breadcrumbs and sautéed.

Menu Makers

• Richly satisfying Classic Turkey Parmesan calls for Italian bread and a simple green salad with Italian herb vinaigrette. Instead of butter to spread on bread, try a dish of extra virgin olive oil for dipping. A dish of Italian brine-cured black olives or ripe olives makes a nice touch.
• Turkey Piccata, with its piquant flavors of lemon, wine and capers, calls for cooked seasonal vegetables: green beans, baby carrots, summer squash or broccoli. To cook, simply sauté any mixture of two or three in olive oil and garlic, then cover pan with lid and steam until just cooked. Boiled red skinned potatoes round out the meal.
• Turkey Schnitzel goes nicely with buttered egg noodles sprinkled with poppy seeds or parsley, braised red cabbage and quickly sautéed spinach. Crisp potato pancakes are an alternative to egg noodles.

Tips and Tricks

• Be sure to use a skillet or sauté pan with low sides. If pan sides are too high, food has a tendency to steam while cooking rather than fry crisply.
• While sautéing scaloppini, shake pan frequently to help keep meat from sticking.
• When frying breaded cutlets, turn with a spatula rather than fork. Using a spatula helps loosen cutlets from the pan bottom and helps keep breading intact.
• Never cover pan while sautéing; moisture will collect quickly and prevent foods from becoming crisp.

SCALOPPINI
RECIPES
S

Classic Turkey Parmesan

- 2 large eggs
- 2 tablespoons 2% lowfat milk or water
- 1 cup Italian-seasoned dry bread crumbs
- ¼ cup all-purpose flour
- ½ teaspoon salt
- ¼ teaspoon freshly ground black pepper
- 1 pkg. The Turkey Store® Breast Slices
- 2 to 4 tablespoons olive oil, as needed
- 3 cloves garlic, peeled, halved
- 1-½ cups prepared spaghetti sauce or spicy spaghetti sauce
- 1-½ cups (6 oz.) shredded mozzarella cheese
- ¼ cup grated Parmesan cheese
- Chopped fresh basil (optional)

Heat oven to 350 degrees. Beat together eggs and milk in a shallow pie plate or dish; place bread crumbs in another pie plate. Combine flour, salt and pepper in a plastic or paper bag. Add turkey slices to bag one at a time; shake to coat lightly with seasoned flour. Dip in egg mixture, letting excess drip off; roll in crumbs to coat lightly.

Heat 2 tablespoons oil in a large non-stick skillet over medium heat. Add garlic cloves; cook 1 minute. Push garlic to edges of skillet. Add turkey slices to skillet in batches (do not crowd) and cook 3 minutes per side or until golden brown and no longer pink in center. Transfer turkey as it is cooked to a 13 x 9-inch baking dish. Repeat with remaining turkey adding additional oil to pan as necessary. Discard garlic; add spaghetti sauce to same skillet. Simmer 2 minutes or until heated through. Spoon over turkey; top with mozzarella and Parmesan cheeses. Bake about 12 minutes or until turkey is hot and cheese has melted. Sprinkle with basil, if desired. *Makes 6 servings.*

Nutrition information per serving: Calories: 361, Protein: 36g, Carbohydrates: 23g, Fat: 15g, Cholesterol: 131mg, Sodium: 1,138mg

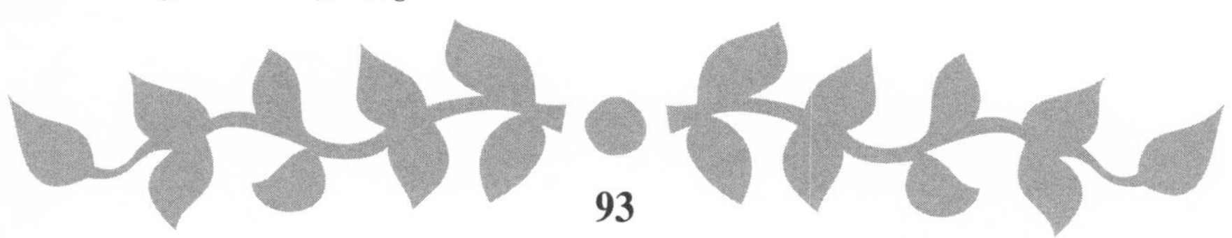

Turkey Piccata

¼ cup all-purpose flour
½ teaspoon salt
¼ teaspoon freshly ground black pepper
1 pkg. The Turkey Store® Breast Slices
1 tablespoon butter or margarine
2 tablespoons olive oil
2 cloves garlic, minced
¼ cup dry white wine or dry vermouth (option: substitute chicken broth)
2 tablespoons fresh lemon juice
¼ cup chopped parsley
2 tablespoons drained bottled capers

SCALOPPINI RECIPES

Heat oven to 200 degrees. In a plastic bag, combine flour, salt and pepper. Add 2 turkey slices at a time to bag; shake to coat. Discard any remaining flour mixture. Heat 1 tablespoon butter and 1 tablespoon oil in a large skillet over medium heat until very hot. Add turkey slices to skillet in one layer (do not crowd pan); cook 1 to 2 minutes per side or until golden brown and no longer pink in center. Transfer to a heat-proof serving platter; keep warm in oven. Repeat with remaining turkey adding 1 tablespoon oil to pan. Add remaining garlic to drippings remaining in skillet; cook 1 minute, stirring occasionally. Add wine and lemon juice to skillet; cook 1 to 2 minutes or until sauce thickens, stirring frequently. Stir in parsley and capers; pour over turkey. *Makes 4 servings.*

Nutrition information per serving: Calories: 247, Protein: 27g, Carbohydrates: 8g, Fat: 11g, Cholesterol: 63mg, Sodium: 378mg

TURKEY SCHNITZEL

2 large eggs
½ cup milk
5 tablespoons all-purpose flour
2 tablespoons grated Parmesan cheese
½ teaspoon salt
¼ teaspoon freshly ground black pepper
⅛ teaspoon nutmeg
3 tablespoons butter or margarine
1 pkg. The Turkey Store® Breast Slices
2 tablespoons fresh lemon juice (optional)
¼ cup chicken or beef broth (optional)

Heat oven to 200 degrees. In a shallow dish or pie plate beat together eggs and milk with a fork. Add 2 tablespoons flour, cheese, salt, pepper and nutmeg; mix well. Melt 1 tablespoon butter in a large non-stick skillet over medium heat until very hot. Place remaining 3 tablespoons flour in plastic bag. Add 2 turkey slices at a time to bag; shake to coat. Dip into milk mixture, turning to coat and letting excess mixture drip off. Add turkey to skillet; cook about 2 minutes per side or until golden brown and no longer pink in center. Transfer to a heat-proof serving platter; keep warm in oven. Repeat with remaining turkey, adding butter to skillet as needed. If desired, after all turkey is cooked, add lemon juice and broth to skillet; boil 1 to 2 minutes, stirring constantly. Pour over turkey.
Makes 4 servings.

Nutrition information per serving: Calories: 339, Protein: 38g, Carbohydrates: 9g, Fat: 17g, Cholesterol: 202mg, Sodium: 586mg

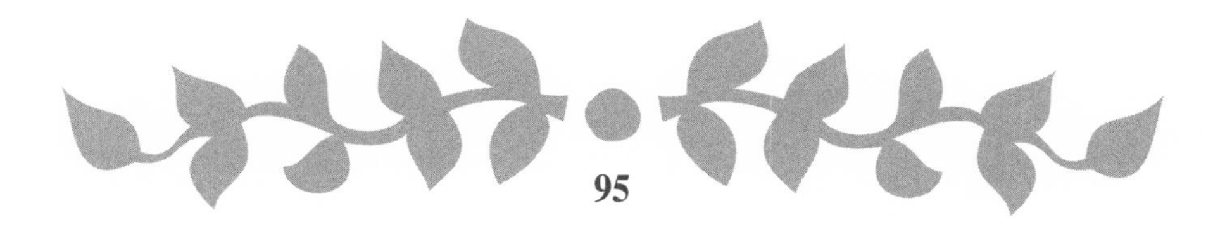

Light Turkey Schnitzel

2 large egg whites
½ cup skim milk
5 tablespoons all-purpose flour
2 tablespoons grated Parmesan cheese
½ teaspoon salt (optional)
¼ teaspoon freshly ground black pepper
⅛ teaspoon nutmeg
Butter flavored cooking spray
3 teaspoons butter or margarine
1 pkg. The Turkey Store® Breast Slices
2 tablespoons fresh lemon juice (optional)
¼ cup chicken or beef broth (optional)

SCALOPPINI RECIPES

Heat oven to 200 degrees. In a shallow dish or pie plate beat together egg whites and milk with a fork. Add 2 tablespoons flour, cheese, salt, pepper and nutmeg; mix well. Coat a large non-stick skillet with cooking spray; add 1 teaspoon butter and place over medium heat until butter sizzles. Place remaining 3 tablespoons flour in plastic bag. Add 2 turkey slices at a time to bag; shake to coat. Dip into milk mixture, turning to coat and letting excess mixture drip off. Add turkey to skillet; cook about 2 minutes per side or until golden brown and no longer pink in center. Transfer to a heat-proof serving platter; keep warm in oven. Repeat with remaining turkey and butter. If desired, after all turkey is cooked, add lemon juice and broth to skillet; boil 1 to 2 minutes, stirring constantly. Pour over turkey.

Makes 4 servings.

Nutrition information per serving: Calories: 230, Protein: 37g, Carbohydrates: 9g, Fat: 5g, Cholesterol: 71mg, Sodium: 228mg

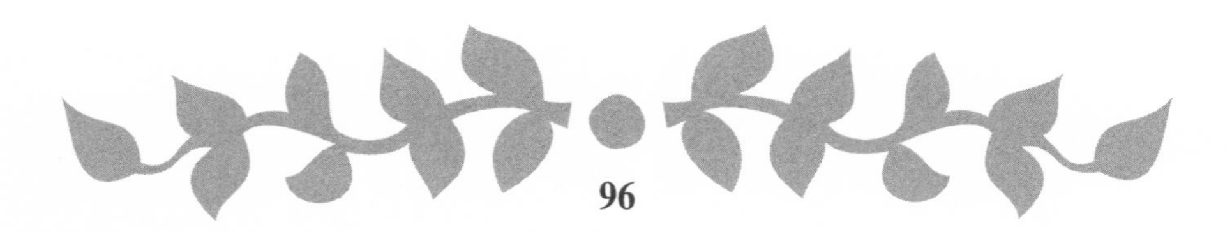

ASIAN RECIPES

Did You Know That?

Nobody knows for sure where chop suey originated, but there are plenty of theories. In The Food Chronology, James Trager suggests that a Chinese dish called tsap seui is native to rural Toisan in Guangzhou, China. Others say there is nothing called chop suey in Chinese cookery, and that it was created in America. According to John Mariani in The Dictionary of American Food and Drink, (although references to it appear in print from 1888 on), one story involves the first Chinese statesman to visit America in 1896. He was asked what he was accustomed to eating and supposedly replied "tsa tsui," Mandarin for "a little of this and that." Reporters translated it as chop suey. Yet another tale involves a dish of leftover meat and vegetables served by a San Francisco cook to a group of drunken miners. Most probably chop suey was created by Chinese cooks who prepared mixtures of meat and vegetables to feed the Pacific railroad workers in the mid-1800s.

Menu Makers

- Szechuan Stir-Fry with rice or vermicelli is a complete meal, containing protein, vegetables and starch. Serve with jasmine tea and end with fortune cookies—another American invention.
- Chop Suey goes nicely with crisp-tender, steamed asparagus that is tossed with a teaspoon of soy sauce and two or three drops of bottled hot chili oil (available in the Asian section of the supermarket).
- For an Asian version of soup-and-sandwich, serve Moo Shu Wraps with bowls of egg drop soup.
- Accompany Asian Grilled Cutlets and the dipping sauce with quickly sautéed snow peas or spinach, curried rice (made from a boxed seasoned rice mix) and bottled mango chutney.
- For a little extra crunch, top Luscious Lo Mein with chopped peanuts and thinly sliced green onion.

Tips and Tricks

- When making wraps with tortillas, it is important to keep tortillas warm and flexible so they will roll without cracking. Heat tortillas according to package directions in microwave or hot dry skillet, then wrap in a napkin until ready to use.
- Most of the work in stir-frying is preparation, not cooking. Chop and store all ingredients in advance.
- Chopping or slicing stir-fry ingredients into similar thicknesses ensures uniform cooking.
- Working with two spatulas, or a spatula and a large spoon, makes stir-frying easier.
- Leftover stir fry? Combine with greens for a flavorful salad or add to broth-based soups.

ASIAN
RECIPES
A

SZECHUAN STIR-FRY

1 pkg. The Turkey Store® Breast Strips
3 tablespoons vegetable oil
1- ½ teaspoons bottled or fresh minced ginger
1- ½ teaspoons bottled or fresh minced garlic
½ teaspoon crushed red pepper flakes
4 oz. shiitake mushrooms, stems discarded, caps sliced, or 1 pkg. (4 oz.) sliced exotic mushrooms
6 oz. snow pea pods, trimmed, halved if large
½ cup thin red bell pepper strips
½ cup low-sodium soy sauce
2 teaspoons cornstarch
2 teaspoons dark sesame oil
3 cups hot cooked white rice or vermicelli pasta
¼ cup thinly sliced green onions

In a medium bowl, combine turkey, 1 tablespoon oil, ginger, garlic and pepper flakes; toss well. Heat remaining 2 tablespoons oil in a large skillet or wok over medium-high heat until hot. Add mushrooms, pea pods and pepper strips; stir-fry 3 minutes. Add turkey mixture; stir-fry 3 minutes. Combine soy sauce and cornstarch, mixing until smooth. Add mixture to skillet; stir-fry 2 minutes or until turkey is no longer pink in center and sauce thickens. Stir in sesame oil; serve over rice or pasta and sprinkle with green onions.
Makes 4 to 6 servings.

Nutrition information per serving based on 4 servings: Calories: 470, Protein: 38g, Carbohydrates: 45g, Fat: 16g, Cholesterol: 60mg, Sodium: 1,312mg

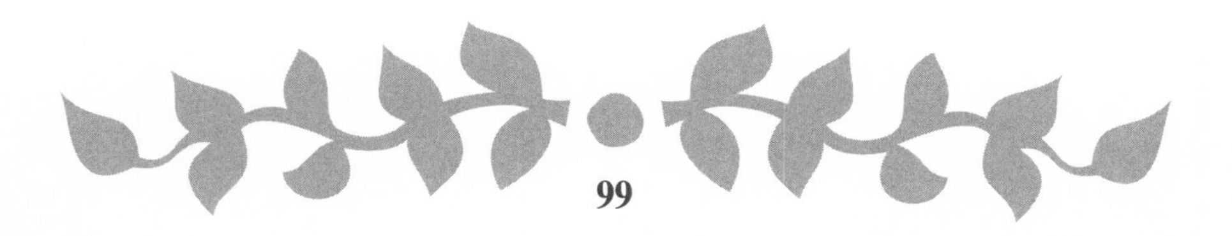

Asian Grilled Cutlets

- ¼ cup soy sauce
- 2 tablespoons dry sherry or sake (option: chicken broth)
- 1 tablespoon dark sesame oil
- 2 teaspoons bottled or fresh minced ginger
- 1 teaspoon bottled or fresh minced garlic
- 1 teaspoon sugar
- ¼ teaspoon crushed red pepper flakes or 1 teaspoon hot chili oil
- 1 pkg. The Turkey Store® Breast Cutlets
- ¼ cup thinly sliced green onions
- ½ teaspoon sesame seeds (optional)

In a shallow dish or plastic bag, combine soy sauce, sherry, sesame oil, ginger, garlic, sugar and pepper flakes; mix well. Add cutlets; turn to coat. Cover dish or close bag securely; refrigerate at least 30 minutes or up to 2 hours.

Prepare barbecue grill. Drain cutlets reserving marinade. Grill over medium coals 3 minutes per side or until no longer pink in center. Meanwhile, bring reserved marinade to a simmer and cook for 1 minute. Stir in green onions. Sprinkle cutlets with sesame seeds, if desired, and serve cooked marinade as a dipping sauce.

Makes 4 servings.

Nutrition information per serving: Calories: 174, Protein: 29g, Carbohydrates: 4g, Fat: 5g, Cholesterol: 53mg, Sodium: 1,117mg

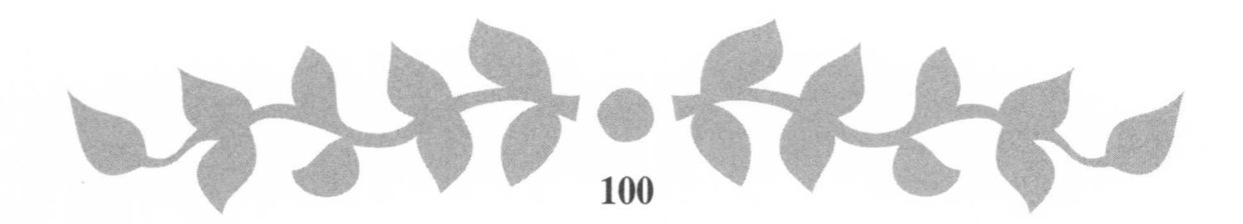

CHOP SUEY

- 2 tablespoons vegetable oil
- 4 oz. shiitake mushrooms, stems discarded, caps sliced, or 2 cups sliced mushrooms
- 2 teaspoons bottled or fresh minced garlic
- 1 pkg. The Turkey Store® Lean Ground
- 3 tablespoons soy sauce
- 1 can (8 oz.) sliced water chestnuts, drained
- 4 green onions, cut diagonally into ½-inch slices
- 1 cup chicken broth
- 1-½ tablespoons cornstarch
- 1 cup mung bean sprouts or broccoli sprouts or radish sprouts
- 3 cups hot cooked white rice or noodles
- ½ cup chow mein noodles

Heat oil in a large deep skillet or wok over medium-high heat. Add mushrooms and garlic; stir-fry 2 minutes. Crumble turkey into skillet; add soy sauce. Cook 4 minutes, stirring occasionally. Add water chestnuts and green onions. Combine broth and cornstarch, mixing until smooth. Add mixture to skillet; simmer uncovered 5 minutes or until thickened. Stir in bean sprouts. Serve over rice; top with noodles.

Makes 4 servings.

Nutrition information per serving: Calories: 532, Protein: 43g, Carbohydrates: 65g, Fat: 12g, Cholesterol: 70mg, Sodium: 1,154mg

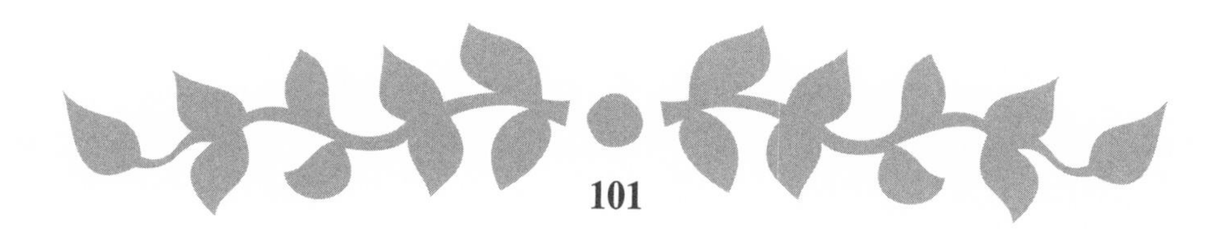

LUSCIOUS LO MEIN

ASIAN RECIPES

- 8 ounces lo mein or udon noodles or spaghetti, uncooked
- 2 tablespoons vegetable oil
- 1 pkg. The Turkey Store® Boneless Breast Tenderloins, cut into ¾-inch chunks
- 2 teaspoons bottled or fresh minced ginger
- 2 teaspoons bottled or fresh minced garlic
- ¼ teaspoon crushed red pepper flakes
- 2 cups sliced bok choy or fresh sugar snap peas
- 1 cup thin red bell pepper strips
- ¼ cup chicken broth
- ¼ cup soy sauce or tamari
- 2 tablespoons oyster sauce
- 2 tablespoons dark sesame oil

Cook noodles according to package directions. Meanwhile, heat 1 tablespoon oil in a large deep skillet over medium-high heat. Add turkey, ginger, garlic and pepper flakes; stir-fry 3 minutes. Transfer to a bowl; set aside. Add remaining 1 tablespoon oil to skillet. Add bok choy and bell pepper; stir-fry 2 minutes. Add broth, soy sauce and oyster sauce; bring to a simmer. Add turkey and sesame oil to skillet; simmer 2 minutes or until turkey is no longer pink in center. Drain noodles; add to skillet and heat through. Serve in shallow soup bowls.

Makes 6 servings.

Nutrition information per serving: Calories: 368, Protein: 36g, Carbohydrates: 35g, Fat: 11g, Cholesterol: 54mg, Sodium: 1,153mg

Moo Shu Wraps

- 2 tablespoons vegetable oil
- 8 oz. shiitake mushrooms, stems discarded, caps sliced
- 2 teaspoons bottled or fresh minced garlic
- 2 teaspoons bottled or fresh minced ginger
- 1 pkg. The Turkey Store® Lean Ground
- 1 red or yellow bell pepper, cut into short, thin strips
- 2 cups cole slaw mix (shredded cabbage and carrots) or sliced napa cabbage
- ½ cup hoisin sauce
- ⅓ cup plum sauce or sweet-and-sour sauce
- 12 (about 7 inch) flour tortillas, warmed

Heat oil in a large deep skillet over medium-high heat. Add mushrooms, garlic and ginger; stir-fry 2 minutes. Crumble turkey into skillet; add bell pepper. Cook 5 minutes, stirring occasionally. Add cole slaw mix and hoisin sauce; stir-fry 3 minutes. Spread a thin layer of plum sauce evenly over each warm tortilla; top with turkey mixture. Fold bottom of tortilla up over filling, fold sides in and roll up.

Makes 6 servings.

Nutrition information per serving: Calories: 438, Protein: 26g, Carbohydrates: 53g, Fat: 15g, Cholesterol: 58mg, Sodium: 864mg

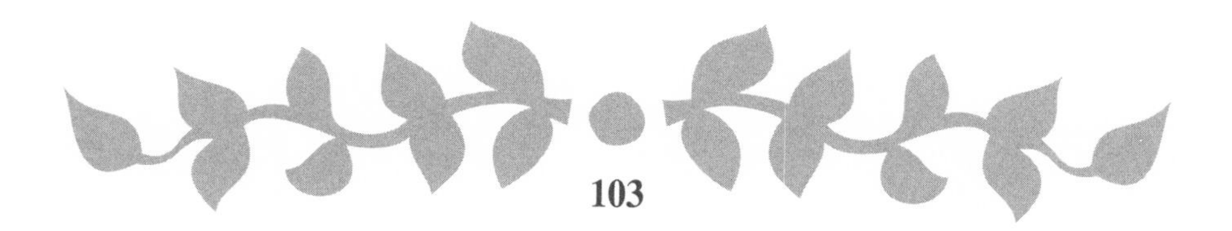

Light Chop Suey

Cooking spray
4 oz. shiitake mushrooms, stems discarded, caps sliced, or 2 cups sliced mushrooms
2 teaspoons bottled minced garlic
1 pkg. The Turkey Store® Extra Lean Ground Breast
3 tablespoons reduced-sodium soy sauce
1 can (8 oz.) sliced water chestnuts, drained
4 green onions, cut diagonally into 1/2-inch slices
1 cup chicken broth
1-½ tablespoons cornstarch
3 cups hot cooked white rice
½ cup chow mein noodles (optional)

Coat a large deep skillet or wok with cooking spray; place over medium heat. Add mushrooms and garlic; stir-fry 2 minutes. Crumble turkey into skillet; add soy sauce. Cook 3 minutes, stirring occasionally. Add water chestnuts and green onions. Combine broth and cornstarch, mixing until smooth. Add to skillet; simmer uncovered 5 minutes or until thickened. Serve over rice; top with noodles, if desired. *Makes 4 servings.*

Nutrition information per serving: Calories: 438, Protein: 43g, Carbohydrates: 61g, Fat: 3g, Cholesterol: 69mg, Sodium: 647mg

KABOB RECIPES

Did You Know That?

Kabob is short for Shish Kebab, Turkey's most famous dish, said to have been created by Turkish soldiers sometime in the 14th century during the Ottoman Empire. The soldiers camped out in tents for long periods and began to grill meat, usually lamb, skewered on their swords over outdoor fires. Marinating the meat was a later refinement. Today, kabobs are composed of a wide variety of meats, poultry, fish, vegetables and fruit—even tofu—all threaded on metal or bamboo skewers.

Menu Makers

• Kabobs make great year-round meals. Barbecue them outdoors on the charcoal grill in warm weather, and broil them indoors in cold or rainy weather. Serve with seasonal side dishes.

• Hickory Barbecued Kabobs can star in a summertime menu with your favorite pasta-vegetable salad. In winter, serve the kabobs with macaroni and cheese and a green salad.

• Tangy Lemon Garlic Kabobs look and taste great with a big platter of sliced ripe tomatoes on a bed of chopped lettuce. Drizzle with ranch dressing and serve with tabbouleh, quickly prepared from a packaged mix. In fall and winter, serve kabobs with a basket of warm pita breads and a Greek salad.

• In summer, serve Honey Mustard Kabobs with potato salad, coleslaw, three-bean salad, and crusty French bread. In winter, serve them with baked beans, winter squash and a mixed green salad with bottled honey-mustard dressing.

• In summer, Mexicali Kabobs—with their bright red and green vegetables—call for warmed corn tortillas, guacamole, and a plate of crisp carrot, cucumber and radish "coins." Add a bowl of bottled ranch dressing for dipping. When cold weather comes, serve with refried beans, shredded iceberg lettuce and chopped tomato salad. Add hot cornbread with butter and honey that has been mixed with a dash of cinnamon.

Tips and Tricks

• If you use a charcoal grill, store unused charcoal in a heavy-duty plastic garbage or lawn bag tightly closed to keep out moisture; dry charcoal ignites faster.

• Rather than use charcoal lighter fluid, purchase a starter chimney available from hardware stores. The chimney ignites charcoal simply with newspaper that you light with a match.

• Place kabobs 1/2 inch apart on the grill or broiler pan to assure even cooking.

• To prevent foods from sticking and to make cleanup faster, spray cold grill or broiler pan with non-stick vegetable oil spray before grilling or broiling.

• Apple, hickory or mesquite wood chips (available where grills are sold) add wonderful flavor to grilled kabobs. Soak chips in water first for at least 30 minutes, drain very well, and sprinkle over lighted charcoals before grilling kabobs.

KABOB
RECIPES
K

Honey Mustard Kabobs

- 1 pkg. The Turkey Store® Boneless Breast Tenderloins, cut into 1-¼-inch chunks
- 1 red bell pepper, cut into 1-inch chunks
- 1 yellow or green bell pepper, cut into 1-inch chunks
- 1 medium red onion, cut into 1-inch chunks
- ½ cup prepared honey mustard barbecue sauce

KABOB RECIPES

Prepare grill or preheat broiler. Alternately thread turkey and vegetables onto 8 (10- to 12-inch) metal skewers or soaked bamboo skewers. Brush half of barbecue sauce over kabobs. Grill or broil about 5 inches from heat source 6 minutes. Brush remaining sauce over kabobs; turn and continue to cook about 8 minutes longer or until turkey is no longer pink in center, turning occasionally. *Makes 8 servings.*

Nutrition information per serving: Calories: 109, Protein: 17g, Carbohydrates: 6g, Fat: 2g, Cholesterol: 33mg, Sodium: 465mg

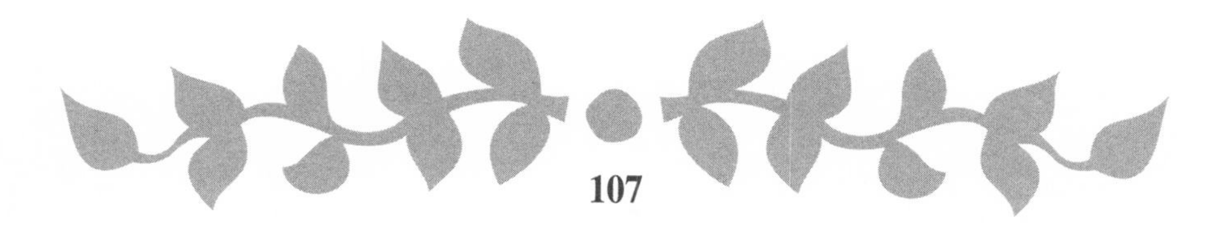

Tangy Lemon Garlic Kabobs

- 18 small red potatoes, about 1-¼ inches in diameter (about 2 pounds)
- 1 pkg. The Turkey Store® Boneless Breast Tenderloins or Lean Boneless Turkey Roast, skinned
- ¼ cup olive oil
- 4 large cloves garlic, minced
- 2 tablespoons fresh lemon juice
- 1-½ teaspoons finely grated lemon peel
- ¾ teaspoon salt
- ½ teaspoon freshly ground black pepper

Wash potatoes but do not dry; pierce each potato with tip of sharp knife. Place in microwave-safe dish and cook at high power 10 to 12 minutes or until barely tender. Rinse in cold water. Meanwhile, cut turkey into 1-1/4-inch chunks; place in large resealable plastic bag. Combine oil, garlic, lemon juice, lemon peel, salt and pepper; add to bag with potatoes. Seal bag, turning to coat. Refrigerate at least 2 hours or up to 8 hours.

Prepare barbecue grill. Drain turkey and potatoes, reserving marinade; alternately thread onto 6 (10- to 12-inch) metal skewers. Grill or broil about 5 inches from heat source 6 minutes. Brush reserved marinade over kabobs; turn and continue to grill or broil 7 to 8 minutes longer or until potatoes are tender and turkey is no longer pink in center. *Makes 6 servings.*

Nutrition information per serving: Calories: 337, Protein: 30g, Carbohydrates: 32g, Fat: 11g, Cholesterol: 53mg, Sodium: 363mg

HICKORY BARBECUED KABOBS

- 1 pkg. The Turkey Store® Boneless Breast Tenderloins
- 3 ears fresh corn on the cob, shucked
- 1 small red onion, cut through core into ½-inch thick wedges
- ½ cup prepared hickory barbecue sauce
- ¼ cup beer (option: substitute non-alcoholic beer)
- 2 teaspoons dry mustard
- 2 cloves garlic, minced

Cut turkey into 1-1/4-inch chunks. Using a large chef's knife, cut corn crosswise into 1-inch-thick slices. Combine turkey, corn and onion wedges in a plastic bag. Combine barbecue sauce, beer, mustard and garlic; pour over turkey and vegetables. Close bag, turning to coat. Refrigerate at least 2 hours or up to 8 hours.

Prepare barbecue grill. Drain turkey and vegetables; discard marinade. Alternately thread turkey and vegetables onto 6 (10- to 12-inch) metal skewers. Grill or broil about 5 inches from heat source 12 to 14 minutes or until turkey is no longer pink in center, turning occasionally.

Makes 6 servings.

Nutrition information per serving: Calories: 176, Protein: 28g, Carbohydrates: 13g, Fat: 1g, Cholesterol: 53mg, Sodium: 187mg

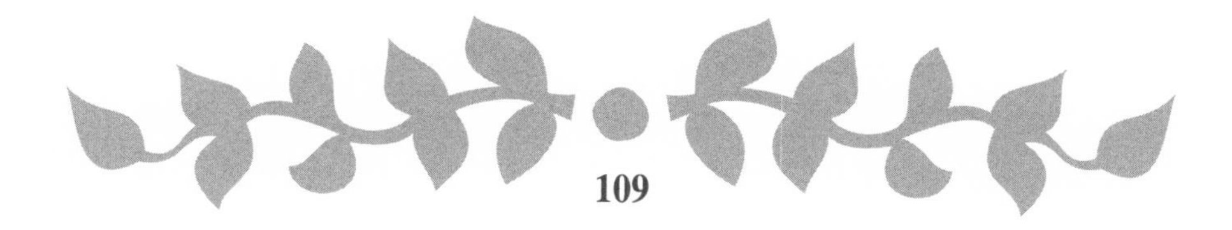

Mexicali Kabobs

- 1 pkg. The Turkey Store® Boneless Breast Tenderloins or Lean Boneless Breast Roast, skinned, cut into 1-¼-inch chunks
- 1 red bell pepper, cut into 1-inch chunks
- 1 green bell pepper, cut into 1-inch pieces
- 2 large green onions, cut into 1-inch pieces
- ½ cup salsa or picante sauce
- 1 tablespoon vegetable oil
- 1 tablespoon honey
- 1 tablespoon fresh lime juice
- 1 teaspoon ground cumin
- 1 teaspoon bottled or fresh minced garlic
- Salt (optional)
- Lime wedges (optional)

KABOB RECIPES

Place turkey, bell peppers and green onions into a resealable plastic bag. Combine salsa, oil, honey, lime juice, cumin and garlic; pour over turkey and vegetables. Close bag; refrigerate at least 1 hour or up to 8 hours.

Prepare barbecue grill. Drain turkey and vegetables, reserving marinade; alternately thread onto metal skewers. Brush with reserved marinade. Grill or broil about 5 inches from heat source 12 to 14 minutes or until turkey is no longer pink in center, turning occasionally. Sprinkle lightly with salt, if desired. Serve with lime wedges, if desired.

Makes 6 servings.

Nutrition information per serving: Calories: 172, Protein: 27g, Carbohydrates: 7g, Fat: 4g, Cholesterol: 53mg, Sodium: 196mg.

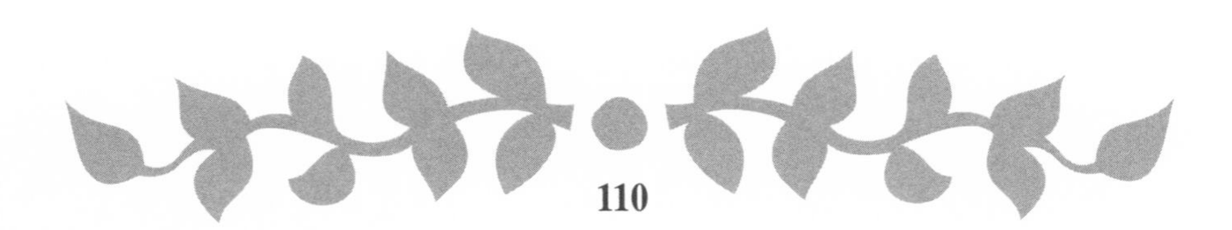

STEW RECIPES

Did You Know That?

Soup or stew? The line between soups and stews is often blurred, especially when it comes to thick, chunky soups. Here's a rule of thumb: some soups may be served as main courses if accompanied by bread or sandwiches and salad. But a stew is too hearty to make a first course. So, if it can be served before the meal as a first course, it's not a stew. Braise or stew? Confusion often arises about the difference between braising and stewing. Braising means to brown meat or poultry, then cook, with the lid on, in just enough liquid to cover, resulting in a thick, reduced, concentrated gravy or sauce. Stewing means to cook meat and poultry, covered, in more liquid than is needed to cover the ingredients, resulting in a thick, soupy liquid that becomes an integral part of the finished dish.

Menu Makers

- New Wave Hungarian Goulash—with its own noodles and vegetables—needs only a loaf of hearty rye bread, butter and a salad made with bottled, roasted red peppers. Drain peppers well and pat dry, then slice into thin strips. Toss to coat with garlic vinaigrette and serve over chopped romaine lettuce.
- Serve Quick Curried Stew over cooked rice or couscous with a fresh fruit salad on the side. A nice presentation: ladle individual portions of stew into big shallow soup bowls and place scoop of rice or couscous on top. Pass chutney, nuts, coconut and cilantro in separate dishes for garnishing.
- Hearty Rustic Stew is truly a one-dish feast. Add a loaf of Italian bread and, for texture, a green salad.

Tips and Tricks

- Because stew is a dish that becomes even better the next day, cook a day ahead, refrigerate covered, and reheat for dinner.
- When stew is refrigerated, any fat that rises to the top will solidify for easy removal before reheating.
- You may also double the recipe and refrigerate half, covered. Plan to reheat for lunch or dinner within three days. Serve different breads and side dishes the second time around. You may also place stew in an oven-proof casserole, top with ready-to-bake refrigerated biscuits, and bake until stew is bubbling hot and biscuits are cooked and lightly browned.

STEW
RECIPES

NEW WAVE HUNGARIAN GOULASH

- 1 tablespoon olive oil
- 1 medium onion, chopped
- 3 cloves garlic, minced
- 1 pkg. The Turkey Store® Lean Polish Sausage
- 1 tablespoon paprika, preferably sweet Hungarian
- ½ teaspoon hot Hungarian paprika or cayenne pepper
- 2 cans (13-¾ oz.) chicken broth
- 1 can (14-½ oz.) stewed tomatoes, undrained
- 1 cup frozen whole kernel corn
- 2 teaspoons dried marjoram or basil
- 1-½ cups (3 oz.) thin egg noodles, uncooked
- ¼ cup sour cream

STEW RECIPES

Heat oil in a large saucepan over medium heat. Add onion and garlic; cook 5 minutes, stirring occasionally. Cut sausage into 1/2-inch slices; remove casings. Add to saucepan; sprinkle with sweet and hot paprika. Cook 2 minutes, stirring occasionally. Add broth, tomatoes, corn and marjoram; bring to a boil. Reduce heat; simmer uncovered 10 minutes, stirring occasionally. Stir in noodles; continue simmering 8 to 10 minutes or until noodles are tender and sausage is no longer pink in center. Serve topped with sour cream.

Makes 6 servings.

Nutrition information per serving: Calories: 275, Protein: 16g, Carbohydrates: 24g, Fat: 14g, Cholesterol: 56mg, Sodium: 1,311mg

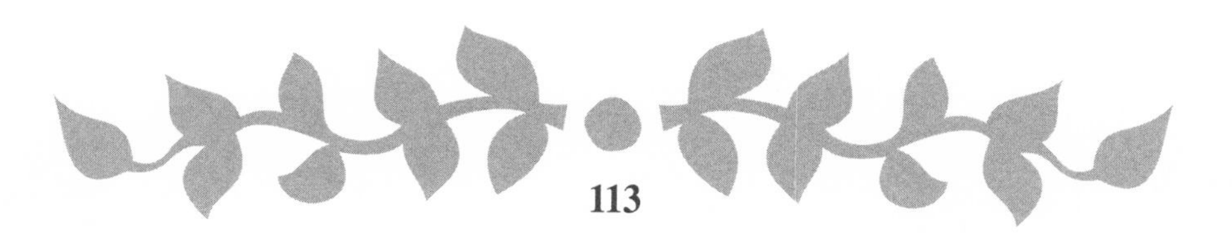

HEARTY RUSTIC STEW

STEW RECIPES

- 4 thick slices smoked bacon, diced
- 3 tablespoons all-purpose flour
- ½ teaspoon salt
- ½ teaspoon freshly ground black pepper
- 1 pkg. The Turkey Store® Boneless Breast Tenderloins or Lean Boneless Breast Roast, skinned, cut into 1-inch chunks
- 2 teaspoons bottled or fresh minced garlic
- 2 cans (13-¾ oz.) beef or chicken broth
- ⅓ cup red wine (optional)
- 1-¼ lbs. small red potatoes, halved
- 8 ounces baby carrots
- 1 cup thickly sliced celery
- 4 oz. shallots or small boiling onions, peeled
- 2 teaspoons herbes de Provence or dried thyme
- 1 tablespoon butter or margarine
- 8 oz. cremini, button or small portobello mushrooms, halved

Cook bacon in a Dutch oven over medium heat until crisp, stirring occasionally. Transfer with slotted spoon to a medium bowl; set aside. Meanwhile, in a plastic or paper bag combine flour, salt and pepper. Add half of turkey, shaking to coat. Transfer mixture to drippings in Dutch oven; cook 5 minutes, stirring occasionally. Transfer to bowl with bacon. Repeat with remaining turkey; transfer to bowl. Add garlic to Dutch oven; cook 1 minute. Add broth and wine, if desired; bring to a boil, scraping up browned bits on bottom of Dutch oven. Stir in potatoes, carrots, celery, shallots and herbes de Provence; return to a boil. Reduce heat; cover and simmer 20 to 25 minutes or until vegetables are almost tender. Meanwhile, melt butter in a skillet over medium-high heat. Add mushrooms; cook 5 minutes, stirring occasionally. Stir into stew along with reserved turkey and bacon mixture. Return to a simmer; simmer uncovered 10 minutes or until turkey is no longer pink in center and stew has thickened slightly.

Makes 6 servings.

Nutrition information per serving: Calories: 374, Protein: 35g, Carbohydrates: 34g, Fat: 11g, Cholesterol: 70mg, Sodium: 1,068mg

QUICK CURRIED STEW

2 tablespoons all-purpose flour
1 tablespoon curry powder
¾ teaspoon salt
¼ teaspoon cayenne pepper
1 pkg. The Turkey Store® Boneless Breast Tenderloins, cut into ¾-inch chunks
3 tablespoons butter, margarine or vegetable oil
1 cup coarsely chopped onion
2 teaspoons bottled or fresh minced garlic
1 lb. (4 cups) assorted cut vegetables or 1 pkg. frozen mixed vegetable medley including broccoli, red bell peppers and cauliflower, thawed
1 cup canned chicken broth
⅓ cup golden or dark raisins
Optional condiments: mango chutney, chopped peanuts, toasted sliced or slivered almonds, shredded coconut and chopped cilantro

In a plastic or paper bag, combine flour, curry powder, salt and cayenne. Add turkey; shake to coat. Melt 1 tablespoon butter in a large deep skillet over medium heat. Add half of turkey; cook 3 minutes or just until outside edges are no longer pink, turning occasionally. Transfer to a bowl; set aside. Repeat with 1 tablespoon butter and remaining turkey. Melt remaining 1 tablespoon butter in same skillet. Add onion and garlic; cook 4 minutes, stirring occasionally. Add vegetables, broth and raisins; bring to a simmer. Cover and cook 5 minutes. Stir in reserved turkey and any accumulated juices from bowl. Cover and simmer 5 minutes or until turkey is no longer pink in center and stew thickens. Serve with condiments as desired.

Makes 6 servings.

Nutrition information per serving: Calories: 238, Protein: 27g, Carbohydrates: 17g, Fat: 8g, Cholesterol: 64mg, Sodium: 588mg

LIGHT HEARTY RUSTIC STEW

STEW RECIPES

- 4 slices turkey bacon, diced
- Cooking spray
- 3 tablespoons all-purpose flour
- ½ teaspoon salt (optional)
- ½ teaspoon freshly ground black pepper
- 1 pkg. The Turkey Store® Boneless Breast Tenderloins or Lean Boneless Breast Roast, skinned, cut into 1-inch chunks
- 2 teaspoons bottled or fresh minced garlic
- 2 cans (13-¾ oz. each) fat free, reduced sodium beef or chicken broth
- ⅓ cup red wine (optional)
- 2 teaspoons herbes de Provence or dried thyme
- 1-¼ lbs. small red potatoes, halved
- 8 oz. baby carrots
- 1 cup thickly sliced celery
- 4 oz. shallots or small boiling onions, peeled
- 8 oz. cremini or button mushrooms, halved

Cook bacon in a Dutch oven over medium heat until crisp, stirring occasionally. Transfer with slotted spoon to a medium bowl; set aside. Coat Dutch oven with cooking spray. Meanwhile, in a plastic or paper bag, combine flour, salt and pepper. Add half of turkey, shaking to coat. Transfer mixture to skillet; cook 5 minutes, stirring occasionally. Transfer to bowl with bacon. Repeat with cooking spray and remaining half of turkey; transfer to bowl. Add garlic to Dutch oven; cook 1 minute. Add broth, herbes de Provence and wine, if desired; bring to a boil. Stir in potatoes, carrots, celery and shallots; return to a boil. Reduce heat; cover and simmer 20 to 25 minutes or until vegetables are almost tender. Meanwhile, coat a non-stick skillet with cooking spray; heat over medium-high heat. Add mushrooms; cook 5 minutes, stirring occasionally. Stir into stew along with reserved turkey and bacon mixture. Return to a simmer; simmer uncovered 10 minutes or until turkey is no longer pink in center and stew has thickened slightly.

Makes 6 servings.

Nutrition information per serving: Calories: 301, Protein: 35g, Carbohydrates: 34g, Fat: 3g, Cholesterol: 60mg, Sodium: 459mg

FOOD FOR THOUGHT

ONE DISH MEAL RECIPES

Did You Know That?

Some of our favorite casseroles have rich histories. For example, Tetrazzini was named in honor of famous opera star Luisa Tetrazzini—nearly 100 years ago—when legendary French chef Auguste Escoffier created the pasta dish for her. Shepherd's Pie—ground or chopped lamb and vegetables covered with mashed potatoes—was a familiar dish in English and Irish pubs. Soon, other meats were substituted for lamb and, in this country, it became an easy way to use up leftovers from the traditional Sunday dinner roast. The tuna noodle casserole, made with condensed cream of mushroom soup and topped with crushed potato chips, was a favorite casserole for brides during rationing in WWII. It was quick and easy and meatless.

Menu Makers

- Serve savory Shepherd's Pie with warm garlic bread and a green salad.
- Turkey Pot Pie is complemented by individual salads of sliced ripe tomatoes and drained, quartered artichokes from a jar on lettuce leaves.
- Turkey Tetrazzini goes nicely with a Caesar salad. Use packaged croutons and bottled Caesar dressing.
- Serve Barbecued Bean Skillet with warm flour tortillas or hot corn bread and coleslaw or grated carrot-raisin salad. Serve with a dish of non-fat sour cream and grated cheddar cheese for optional garnish. Offer bottled red pepper sauce.
- Accompany Noodle Casserole Supreme with a salad of sliced or diced seasonal fruit on lettuce drizzled with bottled poppy seed dressing.

Tips and Tricks

- To be sure that pot pies and casseroles don't bubble over onto the oven bottom during baking, use a pan underneath. Set round casseroles on a pizza pan and rectangular casseroles on a baking tray to catch drips. Before removing from the oven, check for doneness. If necessary, add 5 or 10 minutes to the cooking time.
- To give mashed potato toppings an interesting texture, before baking, draw a dinner fork across the top in one direction, then repeat at right angles to make a cross-hatch design.
- To toast nuts, place in a dry skillet over medium heat. Turn with spatula or stir constantly until nuts begin to brown. Transfer immediately to a plate lined with paper towels to cool. Remember: nuts go quickly from browned to burned.

ONE DISH
RECIPES

SHEPHERD'S PIE

- 1 tablespoon vegetable oil
- 2 teaspoons bottled or fresh minced garlic
- 1 pkg. The Turkey Store® Lean Ground
- ½ teaspoon dried basil
- ½ teaspoon dried thyme
- ½ teaspoon salt
- ½ teaspoon freshly ground black pepper
- 1 can (10-½ oz.) or jar (12 oz.) turkey gravy
- ½ cup frozen corn kernels
- ½ cup frozen tiny peas
- 2-½ cups prepared mashed potatoes, homemade or frozen prepared
- ½ cup (2 oz.) shredded cheddar cheese

ONE DISH RECIPES

Heat oil in a 10-inch oven-proof skillet over medium-high heat. (If skillet is not oven-proof, wrap handle in double thickness of aluminum foil.) Add garlic. Crumble turkey into skillet; sprinkle with herbs, salt and pepper. Cook 5 minutes or until no longer pink, stirring occasionally. Add gravy, corn and peas; simmer uncovered 5 minutes or until vegetables are defrosted and mixture is very hot. Spoon mashed potatoes around edges of mixture, leaving a 3-inch opening in center. Sprinkle cheese over all. Transfer skillet to broiler and broil about 4 to 5 inches from heat source for 2 to 3 minutes or until cheese is melted and mixture is bubbly.
Makes 6 servings.

Nutrition information per serving: Calories: 306, Protein: 26g, Carbohydrates: 23g, Fat: 14g, Cholesterol: 71mg, Sodium: 868mg

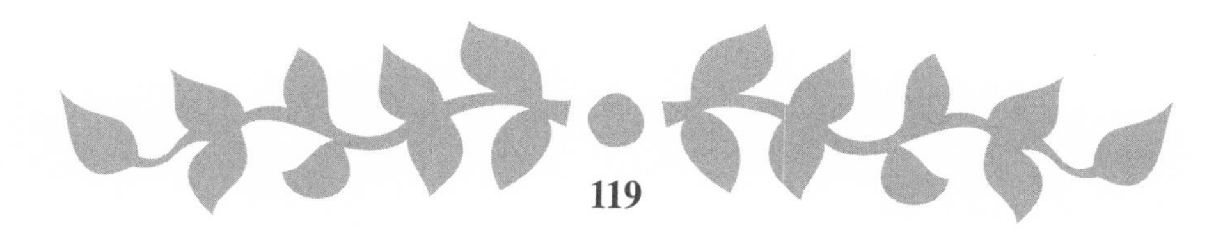

TURKEY POT PIE

- 2 tablespoons butter or margarine
- 1 cup chopped onion
- 3 tablespoons all-purpose flour
- 1-¼ teaspoons salt
- ¼ teaspoon freshly ground black pepper or ground white pepper
- 1 pkg. The Turkey Store® Breast Strips
- ¾ cup whipping cream or half-and-half
- 1 pkg. (10 oz.) frozen mixed vegetables, thawed, or 2 cups chopped cooked vegetables
- ¼ cup chopped parsley or chives (optional)
- Single pastry crust for a 9- or 10-inch pie
- 1 large egg, well-beaten

ONE DISH RECIPES

Heat oven to 400 degrees. Melt butter in a large deep skillet over medium-high heat. Add onion; cook 5 minutes, stirring occasionally. Place flour, salt and pepper in a plastic or paper bag. Add turkey; shake to coat. Add to skillet; cook 2 minutes, stirring occasionally. Add cream; mix well. Add vegetables; simmer uncovered 5 minutes (mixture will be very thick). Remove from heat; stir in parsley. Transfer mixture to a 10-inch deep dish pie plate or quiche dish. Cut 4 slits in pastry to allow steam to escape. Place pastry over dish; seal edges. Brush egg lightly over pastry. Bake 25 to 30 minutes or until pastry is golden brown and mixture is bubbly. Let stand 5 minutes before serving.

Makes 6 servings.

Nutrition information per serving: Calories: 441, Protein: 22g, Carbohydrates: 30g, Fat: 26g, Cholesterol: 129mg, Sodium: 713mg

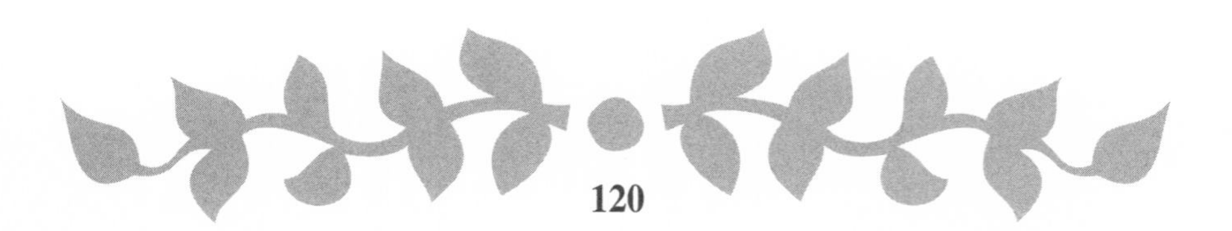

TURKEY TETRAZZINI

- 1 pkg. The Turkey Store® Boneless Breast Tenderloins
- 3 tablespoons all-purpose flour
- 1 teaspoon salt
- 1 teaspoon paprika
- ½ teaspoon freshly ground black pepper
- 3 tablespoons butter or margarine
- ⅓ cup sliced shallots or chopped onion
- 8 oz. sliced cremini or exotic mushrooms
- 2 cloves garlic, minced
- 2 tablespoons brandy (optional)
- 1-½ cups half-and-half or whole milk
- 1 tablespoon chopped fresh thyme or 1 teaspoon dried thyme
- 12 oz. spaghetti or whole wheat spaghetti, cooked and drained
- ¼ cup grated Parmesan cheese
- ¼ cup pine nuts or sliced almonds, toasted

Cut tenderloins into 3/4-inch chunks. Place flour, salt, paprika and pepper in a plastic or paper bag. Melt 1 tablespoon butter in a large deep non-stick skillet over medium-high heat. Add half of turkey to bag; shake to coat. Add to skillet and cook 3 to 4 minutes or until golden brown, turning occasionally. Transfer to a bowl; set aside. Repeat with 1 tablespoon butter and remaining turkey using all of flour mixture. Melt remaining 1 tablespoon butter in skillet. Add shallots, mushrooms and garlic; cook 5 minutes, stirring occasionally. If desired, stir in brandy; cook 1 minute. Add half-and-half and thyme to skillet; bring to a boil. Stir in reserved turkey; simmer 5 minutes or until turkey is no longer pink in center and mixture has thickened, stirring occasionally. Transfer spaghetti to serving plates. Spoon turkey mixture over spaghetti; sprinkle with cheese and pine nuts.
Makes 6 servings.

Nutrition information per serving: Calories: 508, Protein: 37g, Carbohydrates: 46g, Fat: 18g, Cholesterol: 92mg, Sodium: 631mg

BARBECUED BEAN SKILLET

- 1 tablespoon vegetable oil
- 1 pkg. The Turkey Store® Lean Burger Patties
- 1 cup chopped onion
- 1 yellow, red or green bell pepper, chopped
- 1 jar (18 oz.) or can (16 oz.) baked beans, undrained
- 1 can (15-½ oz.) butter beans, drained
- ⅓ cup packed light brown sugar
- ⅓ cup catsup
- 1 tablespoon cider or rice vinegar

Heat oil in a large deep skillet over medium-high heat. Add patties to skillet; cook 2 minutes. Reduce heat to medium; turn patties and continue cooking 2 minutes or until golden brown. Transfer to a plate; set aside. Add onion and bell pepper to skillet; cook 5 minutes, stirring occasionally. Add baked beans, butter beans, brown sugar, catsup and vinegar to skillet; bring to a simmer. Simmer uncovered 10 minutes; top with patties. Continue cooking 3 minutes or until patties are no longer pink in center.

Makes 4 servings.

Nutrition information per serving: Calories: 519, Protein: 36g, Carbohydrates: 69g, Fat: 14g, Cholesterol: 74mg, Sodium: 1,140mg

NOODLE CASSEROLE

- ¼ cup all-purpose flour
- ¾ teaspoon salt
- ½ teaspoon freshly ground black pepper
- 1 pkg. The Turkey Store® Boneless Breast Tenderloins
- 3 tablespoons butter or margarine
- ½ cup chopped onion
- ½ cup sliced celery
- ¼ cup dry sherry (option: chicken broth)
- 1 cup half-and-half
- 6 oz. egg noodles, cooked and drained
- 1 cup frozen tiny peas, thawed
- 1 cup frozen corn kernels, thawed
- ½ cup fresh bread crumbs
- ¼ cup grated Parmesan cheese

ONE DISH RECIPES

Heat oven to 375 degrees. In a plastic bag, combine flour, salt and pepper. Cut tenderloins into 3/4-inch chunks; add to bag, shaking to coat. In a large deep non-stick skillet, melt 2 tablespoons butter over medium heat. Add onion and celery; cook 5 minutes, stirring occasionally. Add turkey; cook 5 minutes, stirring occasionally. Add sherry; cook 2 minutes. Add half-and-half; simmer uncovered 5 minutes or until turkey is no longer pink in center and sauce has thickened. Stir in noodles, peas and corn. Transfer mixture to a greased 13 x 9-inch baking dish. Melt remaining 1 tablespoon butter. Combine bread crumbs, cheese and melted butter; sprinkle over top of casserole. Bake 25 to 30 minutes or until crumbs are golden brown and mixture is bubbly. *Makes 6 servings.*

Nutrition information per serving: Calories: 345, Protein: 27g, Carbohydrates: 35g, Fat: 11g, Cholesterol: 83mg, Sodium: 534mg

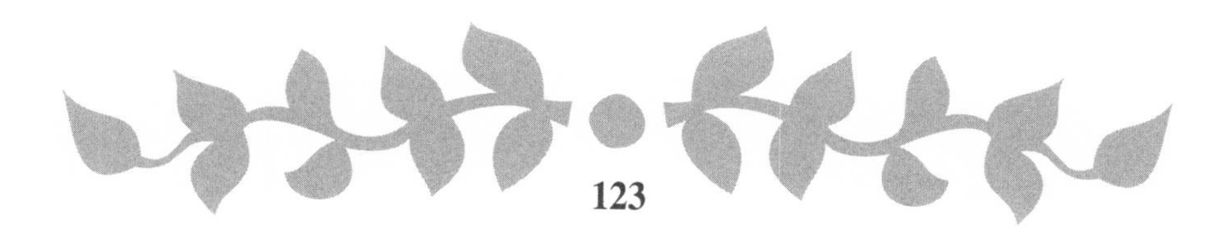

LIGHT SHEPHERD'S PIE

ONE DISH RECIPES

- Cooking spray
- 2 teaspoons bottled or fresh minced garlic
- 1 pkg. The Turkey Store® Extra Lean Ground Breast
- 1 teaspoon herbes de Provence or ½ teaspoon dried basil and ½ teaspoon thyme
- ½ teaspoon salt (optional)
- ½ teaspoon freshly ground black pepper
- 1 jar (12 oz.) fat-free turkey gravy
- ½ cup frozen corn kernels
- ½ cup frozen tiny peas
- 2-½ cups prepared frozen mashed potatoes using skim milk
- ½ cup (2 oz.) shredded low-fat cheddar cheese

Coat a 10-inch oven-proof skillet with cooking spray. (If skillet is not oven-proof, wrap handle in double thickness of aluminum foil.) Place over medium-high heat; add garlic. Crumble turkey into skillet; sprinkle with herbes de Provence, salt and pepper. Cook 5 minutes or until no longer pink, stirring occasionally. Add gravy, corn and peas; simmer uncovered 5 minutes or until vegetables are defrosted and mixture is very hot. Spoon mashed potatoes around edges of mixture leaving a 3-inch opening in center. Transfer skillet to broiler and broil about 4 to 5 inches from heat source for 2 to 3 minutes or until mixture is bubbly. Sprinkle with cheese; return to broiler and broil 1 minute or until cheese is melted.

Makes 6 servings.

Nutrition information per serving: Calories: 238, Protein: 30g, Carbohydrates: 21g, Fat: 5g, Cholesterol: 53mg, Sodium: 565mg

FOOD FOR THOUGHT

ROAST RECIPES

Did You Know That?

Roasting was probably the first cooking method used by man, according to Reay Tannahill in Food In History. Before the discovery of fire, around 500,000 B.C., man ate all his food raw. Roasting is the only cooking method that does not require a cooking vessel and pottery cooking containers came tens of thousands of years later. Tannahill suggests that roasting was discovered when some prehistoric person accidentally dropped a piece of meat in the fire and couldn't get it out for some time. When the meat was finally retrieved, mankind tasted its first roast and no doubt gave it four stars compared to raw meat.

Menu Makers

• Garlic & Lemon Roast Turkey With Potatoes needs a loaf of sliced French bread to spread the roasted garlic on and a tossed salad of mixed baby greens.
• Savory Herb Roasted Turkey Breast & Vegetables has everything but a green vegetable. Serve it with ready-to-use fresh broccoli florets, sautéed in olive oil and garlic, then steamed until tender in a covered skillet. A basket of warm whole grain rolls rounds out the menu.
• Orange Glazed Roast & Vegetables has Asian flavors that would be complemented by a curried rice pilaf made from a package. Add 1/4 cup golden raisins or chopped dried apricots and 1/4 cup slivered almonds to the mix before cooking.
• Thanksgiving Dinner For Six offers a chance to serve all your favorite holiday sides. Start with a relish tray of pickles, olives, radishes and herb cream cheese-stuffed celery. Try baked instead of candied sweet potatoes; put potatoes in the preheated oven on an upper shelf 15 minutes before the roast. Add homemade or instant mashed potatoes, steamed green beans mixed with sautéed mushrooms. End the feast with pumpkin pie. If you have a taste for turkey and stuffing any time of the year, it's easy to make with this simple recipe.

Tips and Tricks

• During cooking, juices gravitate to the center of the roast. During resting, juices gradually distribute throughout the roast. Always let a roast rest tented with foil to keep warm for at least 10 minutes before carving. This preserves juiciness and texture.
• The size of the roasting pan is important. Choose a pan just large enough to hold the roast (and other ingredients) with sides low enough to allow oven heat to circulate around the roast. If the pan is too large, the juices will evaporate or burn. If the pan is too small or the sides too high, the roast will be crowded and have a tendency to steam.

ROAST
RECIPES
R

GARLIC & LEMON ROAST TURKEY WITH POTATOES

- 1 pkg. The Turkey Store® Lean Boneless Breast Roast
- 3 large russet potatoes, scrubbed
- ½ cup canned chicken broth
- ⅓ cup olive oil
- ¼ cup fresh lemon juice
- 1 whole head garlic
- 1 teaspoon paprika
- 1 teaspoon salt
- ½ teaspoon freshly ground black pepper

Heat oven to 375 degrees. Place roast in 9-inch square baking pan. Cut potatoes lengthwise into 6 wedges; arrange skin side down in 15 x 10-inch jelly roll pan or shallow roasting pan. Combine broth, oil, and lemon juice. Separate garlic into cloves. Peel and mince four of the cloves and add to broth mixture. Scatter remaining unpeeled cloves around roast. Spoon 1/3 cup broth mixture evenly over roast; spoon remaining broth mixture over potatoes. Combine paprika, salt and pepper; sprinkle over roast and potatoes.

Bake 40 minutes. Baste roast and potatoes with pan juices. Continue baking 20 to 30 minutes or until thermometer in roast pops up and potatoes are tender. Transfer roast to carving board; tent with foil and let stand 10 minutes before carving. Transfer garlic cloves to a small bowl; cool. Keep potatoes warm in turned-off oven. Carve roast into thin slices; drizzle with pan juices. Squeeze softened garlic cloves from skins; serve with roast and potatoes or use as a spread for French bread. *Makes 6 servings.*

Nutrition information per serving: Calories: 361, Protein: 27g, Carbohydrates: 19g, Fat: 21g, Cholesterol: 55mg, Sodium: 525mg

SAVORY HERB-ROASTED TURKEY BREAST & VEGETABLES

ROAST RECIPES

- ¼ cup olive oil
- 4 cloves garlic, minced
- 1 teaspoon dried basil
- 1 teaspoon dried thyme
- 1 teaspoon dried rosemary, crushed
- 1 teaspoon paprika
- 1 teaspoon salt
- ½ teaspoon freshly ground black pepper
- 1 pkg. The Turkey Store® Lean Boneless Breast Roast
- 2 lb. medium sized red or Yukon Gold potatoes, scrubbed, quartered
- 8 oz. baby carrots
- 12 large shallots or cipolline onions, peeled

Heat oven to 375 degrees. Combine oil, garlic, basil, thyme, rosemary, paprika, salt and pepper. Place roast in large shallow roasting pan or bottom of broiler pan. Scatter potatoes around roast. Spoon oil mixture evenly over turkey and potatoes, stirring to coat lightly with oil. Bake 20 minutes. Add carrots and shallots to pan, stirring to coat lightly with oil mixture. Return to oven and continue baking 30 to 40 minutes or until thermometer in roast pops up and vegetables are tender. Transfer roast to carving board; tent with foil and let stand 10 minutes before serving. Keep vegetables warm in turned-off oven. Carve roast into thin slices; serve with vegetables and drizzle with pan juices.

Makes 6 servings.

Nutrition information per serving: Calories: 417, Protein: 29g, Carbohydrates: 39g, Fat: 17g, Cholesterol: 55mg, Sodium: 282mg

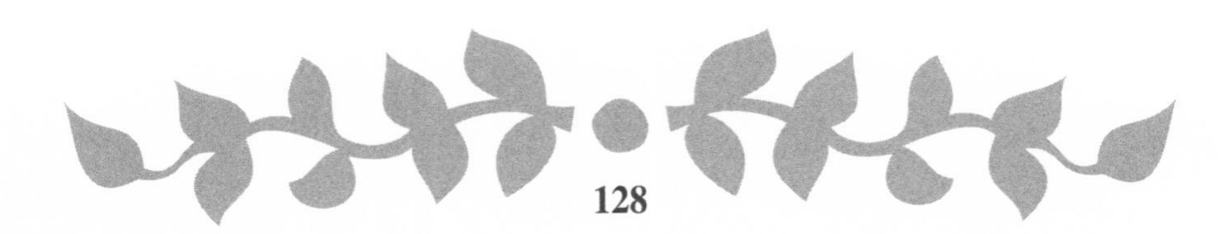

Orange Glazed Roast & Vegetables

- Cooking spray
- 1 pkg. The Turkey Store® Lean Boneless Breast Roast
- ½ cup orange marmalade
- 1 tablespoon seasoned rice vinegar
- 1 tablespoon bottled or fresh minced ginger
- 1 tablespoon Dijon mustard
- 12 oz. baby carrots
- 1 small red onion, cut through the core into ½ -inch-thick wedges
- 8 oz. sugar snap peas
- ¼ teaspoon salt

Heat oven to 375 degrees. Coat a large shallow roasting pan or bottom of broiler pan with cooking spray; place roast in pan. Combine marmalade, vinegar, ginger and mustard; mix well. Spoon 2 tablespoons of mixture over roast. Bake 20 minutes. Toss carrots and onion with remaining marmalade mixture; add to roasting pan. Continue to bake 20 minutes. Stir sugar snap peas into vegetable mixture; continue to bake 10 to 20 minutes or until thermometer in roast pops up. Transfer roast to carving board; tent with foil and let stand 5 minutes before serving. Sprinkle vegetables with salt. Carve roast into thin slices; serve with vegetables.

Makes 6 servings.

Nutrition information per serving: Calories: 297, Protein: 27g, Carbohydrates: 31g, Fat: 9g, Cholesterol: 55mg, Sodium: 310mg

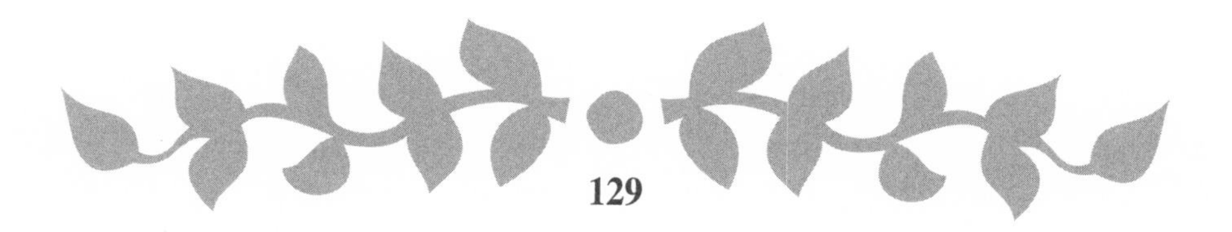

THANKSGIVING DINNER FOR SIX

- 1 pkg. The Turkey Store® Lean Boneless Breast Roast
- 5 tablespoons butter or margarine
- ½ teaspoon each salt, paprika, dried thyme and dried sage
- ¼ teaspoon freshly ground black pepper
- 1 cup chopped onion
- 2 cloves garlic, minced
- 2-¼ cups canned chicken broth
- 1 pkg. (7-8 oz.) herb or cornbread stuffing mix
- ¼ cup dry vermouth (option: substitute chicken broth)
- 1-½ tablespoons all-purpose flour
- 2 tablespoons whipping cream or half-and-half (optional)
- 1 cup whole-cranberry sauce

Heat oven to 450 degrees. Place breast roast in greased oven-proof skillet or small roasting pan. Soften 1 tablespoon butter in microwave oven 25 seconds; rub over top of roast. Combine salt, paprika, thyme, sage and pepper; sprinkle over top of roast. Bake 15 minutes. Reduce oven temperature to 350 degrees and continue to bake 35 minutes or until thermometer in roast pops up.

Meanwhile, melt 2 tablespoons butter in a large skillet or saucepan. Add onion and garlic; cook 5 minutes, stirring occasionally. Add 1-1/4 cups broth; bring to a simmer. Remove from heat; stir in stuffing mix. Transfer to greased casserole dish. For crisp, drier dressing leave dish uncovered; for a moister dressing cover dish. Bake alongside roast during last 20 minutes of roasting time. Transfer roast to carving board; tent with foil. Let stuffing continue to bake 10 minutes. Place oven-proof skillet or roasting pan over burner and turn heat to medium. Add vermouth to pan; scrape and stir with a wooden spoon; cook 1 minute. Melt remaining 2 tablespoons butter in a medium saucepan. Add flour; cook 2 minutes, stirring frequently. Add remaining 1 cup broth and wine mixture from skillet. Cook 5 minutes or until gravy has thickened, stirring occasionally. Stir in cream, if desired. Carve roast into thin slices. Stir any juices from carving board into gravy or stuffing. Serve turkey with stuffing, gravy and cranberry sauce.

Makes 6 servings.

Nutrition information per serving: Calories: 497, Protein: 30g, Carbohydrates: 48g, Fat: 21g, Cholesterol: 83mg, Sodium: 1,220mg

FOOD FOR THOUGHT

SOUTHWESTERN RECIPES

Did You Know That?

A tostada is a crisp flat tortilla used as an edible plate for a variety of toppings. An enchilada is a soft tortilla that is stuffed, rolled and baked with a sauce. A burrito is a stuffed soft tortilla, ends folded and rolled to completely enclose ingredients. It usually has no sauce. A fajita is probably a close Texas relation to the tacos al carbon from Northern Mexico—soft tacos filled with grilled meat. In The Border Cookbook, authors Cheryl and Bill Jamison suggest that in the early days of the state, Mexican-American cowboys were sometimes paid part of their wages in skirt steak and other unwanted cuts of meat—which they cooked over the open fire and, no doubt, stuffed into soft tortillas.

Menu Makers

- Serve burritos, enchiladas and fajitas with several of the traditional Mexican restaurant side dishes: refried beans, guacamole, yellow rice (made from a seasoned package mix) and a salad of shredded iceberg lettuce with chopped tomatoes and a little diced onion.
- Terrific Tostados already have optional refried beans as one of their layers, so serve a side of guacamole and rice.
- Enticing Enchiladas may also be served with a small bowl of soupy black beans over white rice. Top with chopped onion and serve with a lime wedge.
- For a refreshing change, serve a tropical fruit salad combining several of the following: sliced fresh pineapple, mango, papaya, watermelon, kiwi, orange and tiny finger bananas.

Tips and Tricks

- Alternate tortillas: make tostados with blue corn tortillas. Make enchiladas with flavored flour tortillas.
- Leftover tortillas? In addition to cutting into wedges and baking in the oven until crisp for low-fat chips, here are some additional ways to recycle tortillas. Use chips, as they do in Mexican restaurants, to garnish. Stand two or three chips upright in guacamole and refried beans just before serving. To dry tortillas, place on wire racks, uncovered, until they are brittle and can be crumbled into soups or salads. Use two soft tortillas to make quick-and-easy quesadillas. Sprinkle grated cheese over the surface of one and dot with red or green salsa, if desired. Top with a second tortilla. Place on plate and microwave until cheese in center melts. Cut into 8 wedges with kitchen scissors. Make breakfast tostados by topping crisp tortillas with salsa and fried eggs. Dot with non-fat sour cream, if desired. Make breakfast enchiladas by filling soft tortillas with scrambled eggs, topping with salsa and baking until heated through. Sprinkle tops with grated cheese before baking, if desired.

SOUTH-
WESTERN
RECIPES

TERRIFIC TOSTADOS

- 3 tablespoons vegetable oil
- 4 (8-inch) jalapeño-flavored or plain soft flour tortillas
- ½ cup chopped onion
- ½ cup chopped yellow or green bell pepper
- 2 teaspoons bottled or fresh minced garlic
- 1 pkg. The Turkey Store® Lean Ground
- 2 teaspoons ground cumin
- ¾ teaspoon salt
- ¾ cup salsa
- 1 can (15 oz.) refried black beans or refried beans
- 1 cup (4 oz.) crumbled queso fresco or shredded Monterey jack cheese
- ¼ cup sour cream (optional)
- ¼ cup chopped cilantro or sliced green onion

SOUTH-WESTERN RECIPES

Heat 2 tablespoons oil in a large skillet over medium heat until very hot. Add one tortilla to hot oil; cook 1 to 2 minutes per side or until golden brown and crisp. Transfer to paper towels to drain; repeat with remaining 3 tortillas, adding more oil if necessary. Add onion, bell pepper and garlic to oil remaining in skillet; cook 5 minutes, stirring occasionally. Crumble turkey into skillet; sprinkle with cumin and salt. Cook 5 minutes, stirring occasionally. Add 1/2 cup salsa; cook 5 minutes, stirring occasionally. Meanwhile, combine beans and remaining 1/4 cup salsa; heat in microwave oven or small saucepan until hot. Spread bean mixture over tortillas; top with turkey mixture, cheese, sour cream, and cilantro. Serve with additional salsa, if desired.

Makes 4 servings.

Nutrition information per serving: Calories: 606, Protein: 44g, Carbohydrates: 45g, Fat: 29g, Cholesterol: 108mg, Sodium: 1,555mg

ENTICING ENCHILADAS

- 1 tablespoon vegetable oil
- 1 green or red bell pepper, chopped
- ½ cup chopped onion
- 4 cloves garlic, minced
- 1 pkg. The Turkey Store® Lean Ground
- 1 tablespoon Mexican seasoning or chili powder
- 2 cans (10 oz.) mild enchilada sauce
- 2 cups (8 oz.) shredded Mexican cheese blend or Monterey jack cheese
- 12 (7-inch) soft flour tortillas or flavored flour tortillas
- 1 cup shredded lettuce
- ½ cup diced tomato
- ½ cup diced ripe avocado (optional)

SOUTH-WESTERN RECIPES

Heat oven to 375 degrees. Heat oil in a large skillet over medium heat. Add bell pepper, onion and garlic; cook 5 minutes, stirring occasionally. Crumble turkey into skillet; sprinkle with seasoning and cook about 8 minutes or until no longer pink, stirring occasionally. Stir in 1/2 cup enchilada sauce. Remove from heat; stir in 1 cup cheese.

Spread 1/2 cup enchilada sauce over bottom of 13 x 9-inch baking dish. Spoon about 1/3 cup turkey mixture down center of each tortilla. Fold bottom of tortilla up over filling, fold in sides and roll up. Place seam side down in prepared dish. Spoon remaining enchilada sauce evenly over enchiladas. Cover with foil; bake 20 minutes. Sprinkle with remaining 1 cup cheese. Return to oven and bake uncovered 10 minutes or until cheese is melted and sauce is bubbly. Garnish with lettuce and tomato. Top with avocado, if desired. *Makes 6 servings.*

Nutrition information per serving: Calories: 588, Protein: 38g, Carbohydrates: 51g, Fat: 28g, Cholesterol: 113mg, Sodium: 819mg

Buenos Burritos

- 1 tablespoon vegetable oil
- ½ cup chopped onion
- 2 teaspoons bottled or fresh minced garlic
- 1 pkg. The Turkey Store® Breast Strips
- 1 tablespoon Mexican seasoning or 2 teaspoons chili powder plus 1 teaspoon ground cumin
- ½ cup salsa
- 1 can (16 oz.) black beans, rinsed and drained
- 1-½ cups (6 oz.) shredded cheddar cheese or Mexican cheese blend
- ½ cup chopped cilantro or sliced green onions
- 6 (10 inch) soft flour tortillas, warmed

Heat oil in a large skillet over medium heat. Add onion and garlic; cook 5 minutes, stirring occasionally. Toss turkey with seasoning; add to skillet. Stir-fry 2 minutes. Add salsa and beans; simmer about 6 minutes or until turkey is no longer pink in center, stirring occasionally. Remove from heat; stir in cheese and cilantro. Spoon down center of warm tortillas. Fold bottom of tortilla up over filling, fold in sides and roll up.

Makes 6 servings.

Nutrition information per serving: Calories: 482, Protein: 36g, Carbohydrates: 45g, Fat: 17g, Cholesterol: 70mg, Sodium: 921mg

Feisty Fajitas

- 1 tablespoon vegetable oil
- ½ large onion cut into thin strips
- 1 red bell pepper, cut into long thin strips
- 1 green bell pepper, cut into long thin strips
- 2 teaspoons bottled or fresh minced garlic
- 1 to 2 teaspoons bottled or fresh minced jalapeños, as desired
- 1 pkg. The Turkey Store® Breast Strips
- 2 teaspoons ground cumin
- ½ teaspoon salt
- ½ cup salsa or picante sauce
- 8 (7 inch) soft flour tortillas or green chili flavored flour tortillas, warmed
- ¾ cup (3 oz.) shredded Mexican blend cheese or cheddar cheese
- ¼ cup chopped cilantro

SOUTH-WESTERN RECIPES

Heat oil in a large deep skillet over medium-high heat. Add onion, bell peppers, garlic and jalapeños; stir-fry 4 minutes or until crisp-tender. Add turkey, cumin and salt; stir-fry 2 minutes. Add salsa; stir-fry 2 minutes or until turkey is no longer pink in center. Serve mixture in folded tortillas topped with cheese and cilantro.

Makes 4 servings.

Nutrition information per serving: Calories: 450, Protein: 38g, Carbohydrates: 40g, Fat: 16g, Cholesterol: 72mg, Sodium: 972mg

Light Buenos Burritos

- Cooking spray
- ½ cup chopped onion
- 2 teaspoons bottled or fresh minced garlic
- 1 pkg. The Turkey Store® Breast Strips
- 1 tablespoon Mexican seasoning or 2 teaspoons chili powder plus 1 teaspoon ground cumin
- ½ cup salsa
- 1 can (16 oz.) black beans, rinsed and drained
- 1 cup (4 oz.) shredded low-fat cheddar cheese
- ½ cup chopped cilantro or sliced green onions
- 6 (10 inch) fat-free flour tortillas, warmed

Coat a large non-stick skillet with cooking spray; heat over medium heat. Add onion and garlic; cook 5 minutes, stirring occasionally. Toss turkey with seasoning; add to skillet. Stir-fry 2 minutes. Add salsa and beans; simmer about 6 minutes or until turkey is no longer pink in center, stirring occasionally. Remove from heat; stir in cheese and cilantro. Spoon down center of warm tortillas. Fold bottom of tortilla over filling, fold in sides and roll up.
Makes 6 servings.

Nutrition information per serving: Calories: 320, Protein: 32g, Carbohydrates: 37g, Fat: 4g, Cholesterol: 47mg, Sodium: 947mg

LIGHT TERRIFIC TOSTADOS

- 4 (10 inch) soft flour tortillas
  Cooking spray
- ½ cup chopped onion
- ½ cup chopped yellow or green bell pepper
- 2 teaspoons bottled or fresh minced garlic
- 1 pkg. The Turkey Store® Extra Lean Ground Breast
- 2 teaspoons ground cumin
- ¾ teaspoon salt (optional)
- ¾ cup salsa
- 1 can (15 oz.) fat-free refried beans
- 1 cup (4 oz.) low-fat shredded cheddar or Monterey jack cheese
- ¼ cup non-fat sour cream (optional)
- ¼ cup chopped cilantro or sliced green onion

SOUTH-WESTERN RECIPES

Heat oven to 450 degrees. Arrange tortillas on large baking sheet; coat with cooking spray on both sides. Bake 5 minutes. Turn; continue to bake 3 to 4 minutes or until golden brown and crisp. Meanwhile, coat a large non-stick skillet with cooking spray; heat over medium-high heat. Add onion, bell pepper and garlic; cook 5 minutes, stirring occasionally. Crumble turkey into skillet; sprinkle with cumin and salt, if desired. Cook 5 minutes, stirring occasionally. Add 1/2 cup salsa; cook 5 minutes, stirring occasionally. Meanwhile, combine beans and remaining 1/4 cup salsa; heat in microwave oven or small saucepan until hot. Spread bean mixture over tortillas; top with turkey mixture, cheese, sour cream, if desired, and cilantro. Serve with additional salsa, if desired.
Makes 4 servings.

Nutrition information per serving: Calories: 438, Protein: 52g, Carbohydrates: 45g, Fat: 8g, Cholesterol: 79mg, Sodium: 1,068mg

FOOD FOR THOUGHT

STUFFED PEPPER RECIPES

Did You Know That?

The English word "stuffing" replaced the word forcemeat (farcir, French for "to stuff") in 1538. But, according to John Mariani in The American Dictionary of Food and Drink, Victorian-era propriety was offended by "stuffing," so they replaced stuffing with the more delicate term "dressing." Today, stuffing and dressing are used interchangeably. The mild and juicy bell peppers that we love to stuff belong to the same family of capsicum as all the hot peppers: jalapeño, cayenne and habanero peppers, to name a few.

Menu Makers

- If there ever was a complete meal in one package, savory stuffed peppers are it, packing proteins and carbohydrates into a flavorful vegetable cup. All that is needed is salad, bread and a condiment or two.
- Heat a small can of tomato sauce and top Colorful Stuffed Peppers with a spoonful before serving. Add a green salad and rye bread.
- Serve Italian Sausage & Bean Stuffed Peppers with Italian country bread, little dishes of extra virgin olive oil, black and green olives and, if desired, shakers of grated Parmesan and red pepper flakes.
- Serve Moroccan Stuffed Peppers with bottled sweet mango chutney, chopped almonds and cucumbers for topping. Add a basket of warmed whole wheat pita breads.
- Serve Sausage, Potato & Cheese Stuffed Peppers with corn muffins and stewed tomatoes.

Tips and Tricks

- To scrape seeds and membranes easily from inside pepper halves, use a melon baller.
- Add salt to water after it has come to a boil. Salting the water first slows down boiling.
- For easy draining of parboiled pepper halves, boil water in a pot large enough to hold a large sieve or metal colander. Place pepper halves in colander or sieve, submerge in boiling water. When done, merely lift out sieve. To stop cooking completely, rinse parboiled peppers under cold, running water.
- To make sure peppers are dry before stuffing, pat insides dry with clean paper towels.

STUFFED
PEPPER
RECIPES

Colorful Stuffed Peppers

- 4 bell peppers, preferably a mix of yellow, green and red
- 1 tablespoon vegetable oil
- ½ cup chopped onion
- 4 cloves garlic, minced
- 1 pkg. The Turkey Store® Lean Ground
- 2 teaspoons dried basil
- ¾ teaspoon salt
- ½ teaspoon freshly ground black pepper
- 1 can (14-½ oz.) diced tomatoes or seasoned diced tomatoes, drained
- 1-½ cups cooked white or brown rice
- 6 oz. sharp cheddar cheese, finely diced
- ¾ cup fresh bread crumbs, preferably whole wheat or rye
- 1-½ tablespoons butter or margarine, melted
- Paprika (optional)

Heat oven to 375 degrees. Cut peppers lengthwise through stems keeping stem halves intact to hold stuffing. Discard seeds and veins. Cook in boiling salted water 5 to 6 minutes or until crisp-tender; drain well and place cut side up in a 13 x 9-inch baking dish.

Heat oil in a large deep skillet over medium-high heat. Add onion and garlic; cook 5 minutes, stirring occasionally. Crumble turkey into skillet; add basil, salt and pepper. Cook 5 minutes, stirring occasionally. Add tomatoes and rice; continue to cook 5 minutes or until heated through. Remove from heat; stir in cheese. Mound mixture into pepper halves. Combine bread crumbs and butter; sprinkle evenly over filled peppers. Sprinkle with paprika, if desired. Bake about 30 minutes or until bread crumbs are golden brown, filling is hot and peppers are tender. *Makes 4 servings.*

Nutrition information per serving: Calories: 615, Protein: 44g, Carbohydrates: 38g, Fat: 33g, Cholesterol: 144mg, Sodium: 1,016mg

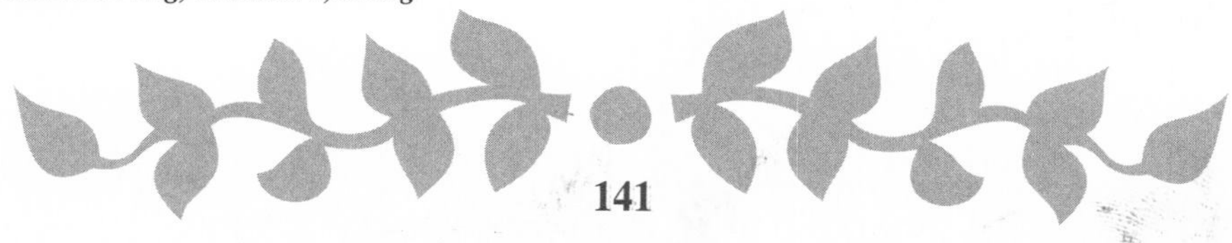

ITALIAN SAUSAGE & BEAN STUFFED PEPPERS

- 4 bell peppers, any color or a combination
- 2 teaspoons garlic-infused or extra virgin olive oil
- 1 pkg. The Turkey Store® Hot or Sweet Lean Italian Sausage
- 1 can (15 oz.) Italian-style or regular tomato sauce
- 2 tablespoons chopped fresh basil or 2 teaspoons dried basil
- 1 can (16 oz.) great northern beans, rinsed and drained
- ½ cup grated Parmesan or asiago cheese

Heat oven to 375 degrees. Cut peppers lengthwise through stems keeping stem halves intact to hold stuffing. Discard seeds and veins. Cook in boiling salted water 5 to 6 minutes or until crisp-tender; drain well and place cut side up in a 13 x 9-inch baking dish. Heat oil in a large deep skillet over medium-high heat. Remove sausage from casings; crumble into skillet. Cook 5 minutes, stirring occasionally. Add tomato sauce and basil; continue to cook 5 minutes. Stir in beans; heat through. Mound mixture into pepper halves. Sprinkle cheese evenly over filled peppers. Bake about 25 minutes or until filling is hot and peppers are tender.

Makes 4 servings.

Nutrition information per serving: Calories: 415, Protein: 30g, Carbohydrates: 35g, Fat: 16g, Cholesterol; 66mg, Sodium: 1,652mg

MOROCCAN PEPPERS

- 4 bell peppers, any color or a combination
- 1 pkg. The Turkey Store® Smoke Seasoned Lean Sausage, Lean Polish Sausage or Lean Bratwurst
- 2 small or 1 large zucchini cut into ¼-inch chunks, diced
- 1-½ teaspoons bottled or fresh minced garlic
- 1 can (13-¾ oz.) chicken broth
- ¼ teaspoon powdered saffron or turmeric
- ⅛ teaspoon cayenne pepper
- ⅛ teaspoon cinnamon
- 1 cup uncooked couscous
- 2 tablespoons chopped mint or basil

STUFFED PEPPER RECIPES

Heat oven to 375 degrees. Cut peppers lengthwise through stems keeping stem halves intact to hold stuffing. Discard seeds and veins. Cook in boiling salted water 5 to 6 minutes or until crisp-tender; drain well and place cut side up in a 13 x 9-inch baking dish. Meanwhile, crumble sausage into a large deep skillet; discard casings. Cook over medium-high heat 5 minutes, breaking sausage into chunks and stirring frequently. Add zucchini and garlic; continue cooking 2 minutes. Add broth, saffron, cayenne pepper and cinnamon; bring to a boil. Stir in couscous. Cover; turn off heat under skillet. Let stand covered 5 minutes or until liquid is absorbed. Stir in mint; spoon into bell peppers. Cover with aluminum foil; bake 20 minutes or until peppers are tender and filling is hot.

Makes 4 servings.

Nutrition information per serving: Calories: 392, Protein: 25g, Carbohydrates: 43g, Fat: 14g, Cholesterol: 83mg, Sodium: 1,207mg

Sausage, Potato & Cheese Stuffed Peppers

- 4 bell peppers, any color or a combination
- 1 pkg. The Turkey Store® Lean Bratwurst, Lean Polish Sausage or Lean Smoke Seasoned Sausage
- 4 cups frozen O'Brien-style potatoes with onions and peppers, thawed
- ⅓ cup thinly sliced green onions
- 1-½ cups (6 oz.) shredded sharp cheddar cheese
- ½ cup catsup
- ½ teaspoon hot pepper sauce

Heat oven to 375 degrees. Cut peppers lengthwise through stems keeping stem halves intact to hold stuffing. Discard seeds and veins. Cook in boiling salted water 5 to 6 minutes or until crisp-tender; drain well and place cut side up in a 13 x 9-inch baking dish. Meanwhile, crumble sausage into a large deep skillet; discard casings. Cook over medium-high heat 8 minutes or until no longer pink, breaking sausage into chunks and stirring frequently. Add potatoes; continue cooking 2 minutes or until heated through. Remove from heat; stir in green onions. Stir in cheese; spoon into peppers. Combine catsup and pepper sauce; spoon over peppers. Bake uncovered 25 minutes or until peppers are tender and filling is hot. Sprinkle with remaining 1/2 cup cheese. Return to oven; bake 2 minutes or until cheese is melted.

Makes 4 servings.

Nutrition information per serving: Calories: 483, Protein: 31g, Carbohydrates: 37g, Fat: 24g, Cholesterol: 101mg, Sodium: 1,307mg

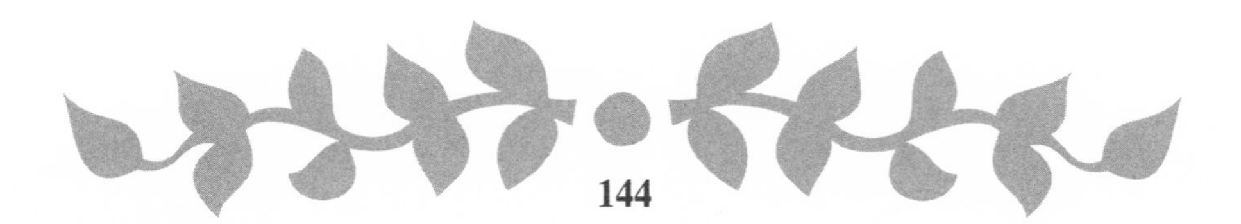

EASY STUFFED PEPPERS

- 4 bell peppers, preferably a mix of yellow, green and red
- 1 tablespoon vegetable oil
- ½ cup frozen chopped onion, thawed in microwave oven 45 seconds
- 2 teaspoons bottled minced garlic
- 1 pkg. The Turkey Store® Lean Ground
- 2 teaspoons dried basil
- ¾ teaspoon salt
- ½ teaspoon freshly ground black pepper
- 1 can (14-½ oz.) diced tomatoes or seasoned diced tomatoes, drained
- 1-½ cups cooked white or brown rice
- 6 oz. sharp cheddar cheese, finely diced, or 1-½ cups (6 oz.) shredded cheddar cheese
- ¾ cup fresh bread crumbs
- 1-½ tablespoons butter or margarine, melted
- Paprika (optional)

STUFFED PEPPER RECIPES

Cut peppers lengthwise through stems keeping stem halves intact to hold stuffing. Discard seeds and veins. Place cut-side down in a 13 x 9-inch microwave-safe baking dish or casserole large enough to hold in one layer. Cover tightly with plastic wrap; cook in microwave oven at high power 5 minutes. Remove from oven; let stand covered.

Combine oil, onion and garlic in a large microwave-safe casserole dish; cook uncovered at high power 2-1/2 minutes. Crumble turkey into dish; add basil, salt and pepper. Cover with lid or vented plastic wrap. Cook 3 minutes; stir well. Cover and continue cooking 2 to 3 minutes or until turkey is no longer pink. Add tomatoes and rice; mix well. Add cheese; mix well. Turn peppers cut side up in dish. Mound turkey mixture into pepper halves. Combine bread crumbs and butter; sprinkle evenly over filled peppers. Sprinkle with paprika, if desired. Cover loosely with wax paper; cook at high power 12 to 15 minutes or until filling is hot and peppers are tender.
Makes 4 servings.

Nutrition information per serving: Calories: 615, Protein: 44g, Carbohydrates: 38g, Fat: 33g, Cholesterol: 144mg, Sodium: 1,016mg

Light Colorful Stuffed Peppers

4 bell peppers, preferably a mix of yellow, green and red
Cooking spray
½ cup chopped onion
4 cloves garlic, minced
1 pkg. The Turkey Store® Extra Lean Ground Breast
2 teaspoons dried basil
¾ teaspoon salt (optional)
½ teaspoon freshly ground black pepper
1 can (14-½ oz.) diced tomatoes or seasoned diced tomatoes, drained
1-½ cups cooked white or brown rice
6 oz. low-fat cheddar cheese, finely diced
¾ cup fresh bread crumbs
Paprika (optional)

Heat oven to 375 degrees. Cut peppers lengthwise through stems keeping stem halves intact to hold stuffing. Discard seeds and veins. Cook in boiling salted water 5 to 6 minutes or until crisp-tender; drain well and place cut side up in a 13 x 9-inch baking dish.

Coat a large non-stick skillet with cooking spray; heat over medium-high heat. Add onion and garlic; cook 5 minutes, stirring occasionally. Crumble turkey into skillet; add basil, salt and pepper. Cook 5 minutes, stirring occasionally. Add tomatoes and rice; continue to cook 5 minutes or until heated through. Remove from heat; stir in cheese. Mound mixture into pepper halves. Sprinkle bread crumbs evenly over filled peppers. Coat with cooking spray; sprinkle with paprika, if desired. Bake about 30 minutes or until bread crumbs are golden brown, filling is hot and peppers are tender.
Makes 4 servings.

Nutrition information per serving: Calories: 432, Protein: 51g, Carbohydrates: 39g, Fat: 10g, Cholesterol: 84mg, Sodium: 605mg

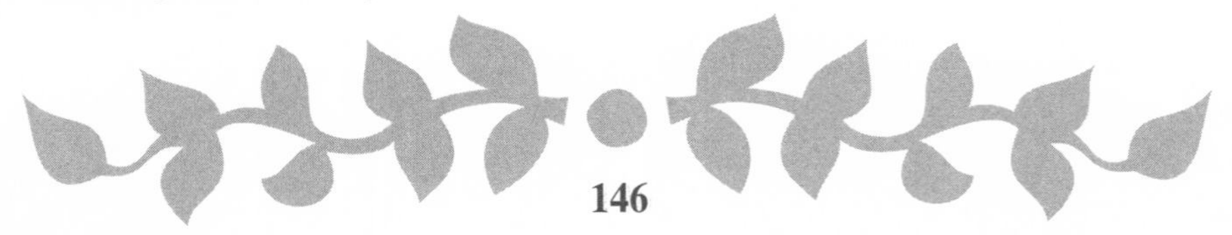

INDEX

Lean Ground

Extra Lean Ground Breast

Lean Burger Patties

Seasoned Lean Burger Patties

Lean Boneless Breast Roast

Boneless Breast Tenderloins

Breast Cutlets

Breast Strips

Breast Slices

Dinner Sausage

Breakfast Sausage

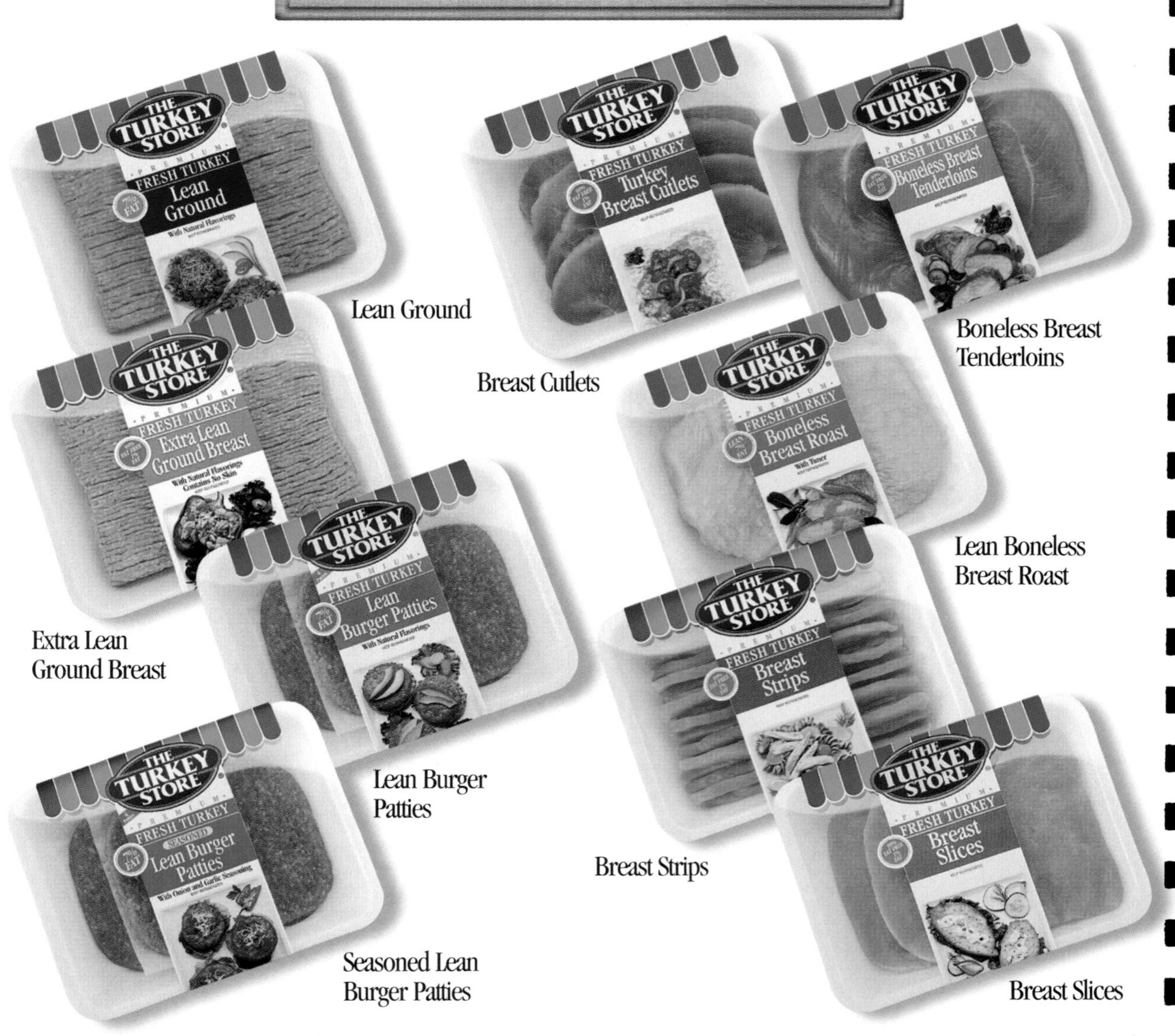

Lean Ground

Breast Cutlets

Boneless Breast Tenderloins

Extra Lean Ground Breast

Lean Boneless Breast Roast

Lean Burger Patties

Breast Strips

Seasoned Lean Burger Patties

Breast Slices

THE TURKEY STORE®

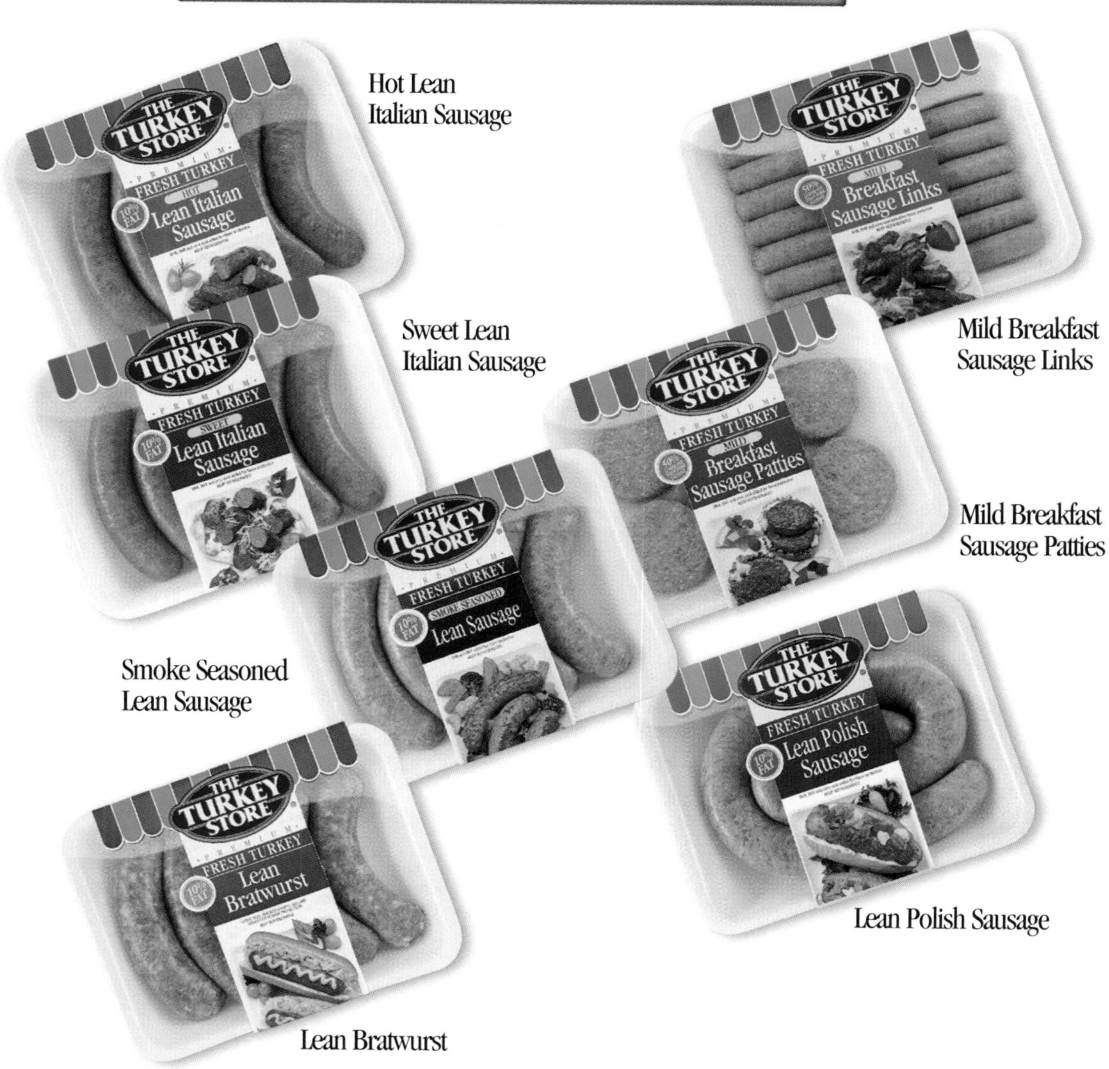
Hot Lean
Italian Sausage
Sweet Lean
Italian Sausage
Mild Breakfast
Sausage Links
Mild Breakfast
Sausage Patties
Smoke Seasoned
Lean Sausage
Lean Polish Sausage
Lean Bratwurst

NUTRITIONAL INFORMATION

RECIPE	Beef or Traditional Meat Cal	Fat	Turkey Cal	Fat
The Best Meatloaf Recipes				
Best Ever Meatloaf	357	23	243	7
Italian-Style Meatloaf	422	34	193	7
Grilled Meatloaf	336	19	261	10
Light Best Ever Meatloaf	279	13	191	2
The Best Spaghetti Recipes				
Homestyle Spaghetti With Meatballs	720	32	565	18
Tex-Mex Spaghetti	808	46	491	18
Spaghetti With Hot Italian Sausage	530	20	491	14
Light Spaghetti With Meat Sauce	486	11	425	4
The Best Burger Recipes				
All-American Cheeseburgers	638	34	566	23
Mexicali Burgers	528	26	450	18
Mouth-Watering Patty Melts	681	43	494	26
Grilled Burgers Supreme	399	19	320	10
Italian Burgers	670	38	498	19
Light All-American Burgers	590	24	378	3
The Best Taco Recipes				
Tantalizing Tacos	510	33	413	20
Chunky Santa Fe Tacos	470	32	343	16
Quick & Easy Tacos	539	36	349	16
Light Tantalizing Tacos	571	30	382	10
The Best Sloppy Joe Recipes				
Traditional Sloppy Joes	487	19	390	13
Spicy Sloppy Joes	530	19	390	6
Italian Sloppy Joes	515	26	457	17
Light Sloppy Joes	373	13	293	2
The Best Sausage Sandwich Recipes				
Sausage, Pepper & Onion Heroes	444	22	398	15
Smoked Sausage Sandwiches With Spicy Kraut Topping	705	44	325	10
Bratwurst & Grilled Onion Hoagies	412	20	378	13
Smoky Spanish Sandwiches	617	39	377	13

RECIPE	Beef or Traditional Meat Cal	Fat	Turkey Cal	Fat
The Best Chili Recipes				
Tex-Mex Chili	326	15	282	10
Smoky Chipotle Chili	450	32	250	11
Quick & Easy Chili	406	14	228	3
Light Tex-Mex Chili	295	12	228	3
The Best Soup Recipes				
Tuscan Bean & Tomato Soup	487	25	331	13
Turkey Noodle Soup	302	15	247	10
Marvelous Mushroom Barley Soup	264	11	209	5
Sausage & Rice Soup	429	32	229	12
Comforting Double Corn Chowder	356	23	323	17
Light Comforting Double Corn Chowder	269	13	235	7
The Best Cajun Recipes				
Smoky Jambalya	555	34	355	13
New Orleans Gumbo	403	25	269	10
Red Beans & Rice	490	15	412	4
Light New Orleans Gumbo	373	23	203	2
The Best Lasagna Recipes				
Classic Lasagna	389	21	360	17
Lasagna Florentine	396	18	346	12
Quick & Easy Lasagna	447	30	409	24
Light Lasagna Florentine	318	10	268	3
The Best Breakfast & Brunch Recipes				
Breakfast Muffin Sandwiches	388	22	414	23
Sausage & Sassy Scrambled Eggs	259	19	317	23
Pigs in a Blanket	442	16	475	18
Huevos Rancheros	476	36	502	37
Fire & Ice Brunch Bake	645	44	458	24
Light Sausage & Sassy Scrambled Eggs	177	10	210	12

NUTRITIONAL INFORMATION

RECIPE	Beef or Traditional Meat		Turkey	
	Cal	Fat	Cal	Fat
The Best Pizza Recipes				
Sausage Pizza	462	22	429	17
Thai-Style Pizza	384	13	347	9
Mediterranean-Style Pizza	496	22	442	18
Light Mediterranean-Style Pizza	354	14	293	8
The Best Salad Recipes				
Asian Noodle Salad	421	16	405	14
Chef's Salad Supreme	722	55	529	32
Grilled Caesar	375	23	309	15
Southwestern Rice Salad	433	19	384	13
Wonderful Waldorf Salad	309	20	255	14
Light Chef's Salad	468	28	277	5
The Best Scaloppini Recipes				
Classic Turkey Parmesan	393	18	361	15
Turkey Piccata	284	14	247	11
Turkey Schnitzel	362	17	339	17
Light Turkey Schnitzel	277	9	230	5
The Best Asian Recipes				
Szechuan Stir Fry	533	23	470	16
Asian Grilled Cutlets	235	15	174	5
Chop Suey	616	25	532	12
Luscious Lo Mein	424	17	368	11
Moo Shu Wraps	483	20	438	15
Light Chop Suey	538	16	438	3
The Best Kabob Recipes				
Honey Mustard Kabobs	215	15	109	2
Tangy Lemon Garlic Kabobs	507	32	337	11
Hickory Barbecue Kabobs	346	22	176	1
Mexicali Kabobs	342	25	172	4
The Best Stew Recipes				
New Wave Hungarian Goulash	444	32	275	14
Hearty Rustic Stew	498	27	374	11
Quick Curried Stew	389	27	238	8
Light Hearty Rustic Stew	471	25	301	3

RECIPE	Beef or Traditional Meat		Turkey	
	Cal	Fat	Cal	Fat
The Best One Dish Recipes				
Shepherd's Pie	399	22	306	14
Turkey Pot Pie	554	40	441	26
Turkey Tetrazzini	565	24	508	18
Barbecue Bean Skillet	573	19	519	14
Turkey Noodle Casserole	459	25	345	11
Light Shepherd's Pie	305	14	238	5
The Best Roast Recipes				
Garlic & Lemon Roast Turkey With Potatoes	390	24	361	21
Savory Herb Roasted Turkey Breast & Vegetables	536	32	417	17
Orange Glazed Roast & Vegetables	326	12	297	9
Thanksgiving Dinner for Six	526	24	497	21
The Best Southwestern Recipes				
Terrific Tostados	743	39	606	29
Enticing Enchiladas	666	39	588	28
Buenos Burritos	524	22	482	17
Feisty Fajitas	620	37	450	16
Light Buenos Burritos	362	9	320	4
Light Terrific Tostados	538	21	438	8
The Best Stuffed Pepper Recipes				
Colorful Stuffed Peppers	682	40	615	33
Italian Sausage & Bean Stuffed Peppers	450	24	415	16
Moroccan Peppers	645	41	392	14
Sausage, Potato & Cheese Stuffed Peppers	504	31	438	24
Easy Stuffed Peppers	682	40	615	33
Light Colorful Stuffed Peppers	531	23	432	10